"Prasanta Verma wonderfully articulates what ethnic loneliness means for people of color through personal stories, poetry, and research. This combination of experiences and expert insights helps us move out of the shadows of subconscious discomfort toward acceptance, healing, and strength. Read this book to grow your appreciation of how our God-given differences add to the richness of living, relating, and belonging."

**DJ Chuang,** director of Christian Asian Mental Health and author of *MultiAsian.Church: A Future for Asian Americans in a Multiethnic World*

"*Beyond Ethnic Loneliness* is a moving read for any person of color who has silently carried the burden of isolation, invisibility, and marginalization in a society that has 'devalued, attacked, beaten, shot, lynched, enslaved, exiled, killed' those who do not conform to a 'white-majority culture.' Prasanta Verma's words provided the embrace I never received in spaces where I felt unseen and unheard when discrimination and racism disregarded my racial identity. If you work with persons of color and seek to comprehend these struggles, read this book now."

**Terence Lester,** founder of Love Beyond Walls and author of *All God's Children*

"Before reading this book, I had never thought to give myself permission to connect my ethnicity with loneliness—even though I experienced it in palpable amounts. Prasanta not only gives readers permission for this and so much more in her offering, but she also holds their hands and walks alongside them as she illuminates a path forward. Belonging is deeply personal and spiritual, and it embodies the gift of community given to us by a relational Savior. I am excited that others will get to explore these topics in *Beyond Ethnic Loneliness* and be reminded of their place in this world and the world to come."

**Quantrilla Ard,** author, speaker, and grief coach at The PhD Mamma

"With clarity and insight, Prasanta Verma gives voice to stories of isolation and marginalization that are often experienced by many immigrants and people of color. Her engagement with these narratives addresses critical issues faced by racial and ethnic minorities. The book also moves the reader forward toward healing, hope, and an understanding of culture and ethnicity that is rooted in Scripture. Verma reminds us of the God who perpetually knows, sees, and loves us. This book is a valuable resource to anyone engaging in issues of race and ethnicity."

**Joshua Joseph,** assistant director of the Thriving Immigrant Congregations Initiative at Trinity Evangelical Divinity School

"Prasanta Verma not only takes readers on her journey as an immigrant to the United States but also does a deep dive into the struggles, blessings, and humorous situations immigrants find themselves in as they live, grow, and try to find their place in a country they have not originated from. She defines the complicated feelings of life in the in-between space while simultaneously reminding ethnic outsiders that not only do they belong, but their ethnicity is also beautiful and God honoring. This book will challenge your assumptions and help you walk in the outsider's shoes."

**E. L Sherene Joseph,** writer and storyteller at the crossroads of Christianity, culture, and community

*"Beyond Ethnic Loneliness* is a literary basket brimming with goodness. Within its pages you will find a sojourner's memoir, a motherly embrace, a valuable glossary, scriptural insight, and thoughtful resources. Loneliness has been a backdrop to our human stories, and this project brings much-needed acknowledgment and practical steps to help fill the emptiness. I'm incredibly grateful to call Prasanta Verma a friend, a sister in Christ, and a leader of wisdom and grace. May her work spread far and wide into the hands and hearts so desperate to know that they belong—to themselves, in safe spaces, and to our God."

**Dorena Williamson,** bridge builder and author of *The Celebration Place*

*"Beyond Ethnic Loneliness* is a revelation. Prasanta Verma beautifully illuminates the joys and struggles of ethnic immigrants and BIPOC in America. Although ethnic loneliness is found inconsistently in other literature on ethnicity, racism, or racial trauma, Prasanta centers it. She skillfully shares this through stories about her family, India, American history, Scripture, research, and poetry. Prasanta invites us on a journey from ethnic loneliness toward embracing who we are and how we belong to God, ourselves, and one another. She also graciously welcomes and teaches us how to walk alongside those on this journey."

**Sheila Wise Rowe,** author of *Healing Racial Trauma* and *Young, Gifted, and Black*

*"Beyond Ethnic Loneliness* so helpfully names and holds space for the challenges faced by ethnic minorities, challenges that are overlooked or swept under the rug. I felt seen by Prasanta Verma's thoughtful reflections, compelling stories, and poignant poetry. She gives insights of Jesus being in the margins with us and how Scripture speaks to and offers hope for our experiences of marginalization. I wish I'd had a book like this much earlier in my life and commend it to anyone looking to learn and grow in this area!"

**Sabrina S. Chan,** author of *Learning Our Names: Asian American Christians on Identity, Relationships, and Vocation* and national director of InterVarsity Asian American Ministries

# BEYOND ETHNIC LONELINESS

*The Pain of Marginalization
and the Path to Belonging*

## PRASANTA VERMA

An imprint of InterVarsity Press
Downers Grove, Illinois

**InterVarsity Press**
P.O. Box 1400 | Downers Grove, IL 60515-1426
ivpress.com | email@ivpress.com

InterVarsity Press® is the publishing division of InterVarsity Christian Fellowship/USA®. For more information, visit intervarsity.org.

All Scripture quotations, unless otherwise indicated, are taken from The Holy Bible, New International Version®, NIV®. Copyright © 1973, 1978, 1984, 2011 by Biblica, Inc.™ Used by permission of Zondervan. All rights reserved worldwide. www.zondervan.com. The "NIV" and "New International Version" are trademarks registered in the United States Patent and Trademark Office by Biblica, Inc.™

While any stories in this book are true, some names and identifying information may have been changed to protect the privacy of individuals.

Published in association with the Books & Such Literary Management, 52 Mission Circle, Suite 122, PMB 170, Santa Rosa, CA 95409-5370, www.booksandsuch.com.

The publisher cannot verify the accuracy or functionality of website URLs used in this book beyond the date of publication.

Cover design: David Fassett
Interior design: Daniel van Loon
Cover image: TanyaJoy / iStock

ISBN 978-1-5140-0741-9 (print) | ISBN 978-1-5140-0742-6 (digital)

Printed in the United States of America ♾

**Library of Congress Cataloging-in-Publication Data**
Names: Anumolu, Prasannata Verma, 1968- author.
Title: Beyond ethnic loneliness : the pain of marginalization and the path
   to belonging / Prasanta Verma.
Description: Downers Grove, IL : InterVarsity Press, [2024] | Includes
   bibliographical references.
Identifiers: LCCN 2023048842 (print) | LCCN 2023048843 (ebook) | ISBN
   9781514007419 (print) | ISBN 9781514007426 (digital)
Subjects: LCSH: East Indian Americans. | East Indian Americans–Cultural
   assimilation. | East Indian Americans–Social conditions. | Ethnic
   relations--Religious aspects–Christianity.
Classification: LCC E184.E2 .A58 2024 (print) | LCC E184.E2 (ebook) | DDC
   305.8914/073–dc23/eng/20231130
LC record available at https://lccn.loc.gov/2023048842
LC ebook record available at https://lccn.loc.gov/2023048843

31  30  29  28  27  26  25  24  |  12  11  10  9  8  7  6  5  4  3  2  1

To my parents, Chander and Kewal,

*your courage took you to a new country*

*and your example inspires me daily.*


To the ones who feel lonely.

# CONTENTS

# Introduction

# A COUNTRY WITH NO NAME

*I long, as does every human being, to be*
*at home wherever I find myself.*

Maya Angelou

G o back to Indiana, or wherever it is you came from!" she
hissed.[1] I cannot recall what preceded her comment, nor
what precipitated her hatred. She didn't like me, and for no ap-
parent reason except one: my skin color.

We were on the softball field for recess. In the outfield, well out
of the teacher's earshot, no one else could hear our conversation.
It was a typically hot, sunny southern day and I could feel the red
clay beneath my feet burning like hot coals. My classmate turned
toward me, her eyes seething with hatred and bitterness.

Sound travels faster in humid air, stinging the ears more quickly
than normal. I said nothing in response but knew what she meant.
Naming a state—Indiana—instead of the country—India—made
her meaning undeniably clear. Or was that simply how little third
graders in rural Alabama really knew? My family was, as far as
we were aware, the only Indian family within a forty-five-minute
radius, and my classmate had never met (or presumably seen)
anyone else from the far-off land of "Indiana."

At that moment, I didn't cry. I didn't tell my parents what my classmate said. In fact, I didn't tell anyone. I felt pushed to the side and felt the loneliness of being different. It wasn't until years later that I began to process and speak of situations like this, times when I felt alone in my experience of being an immigrant or someone who looked different from others.

But where *was* she telling me to return to? I was puzzled. My family had recently moved from South Dakota, so that was the only place that made logical sense in my mind. It did not occur to me to go back anywhere else. I was born in India, so perhaps she thought we had recently clambered off our own canoes from the Gulf Coast and walked north. She didn't know I was one year old when my parents immigrated, that this was the only country I had ever known.

But in my head, I've been going back ever since, trying to find that place called home.

I have never forgotten her words.

My experience that day on the playground opened my eyes, as my classmate clearly told me who I was not. Her words reminded me of what she and others saw when they looked at me. I looked at me and saw "American." Others looked at me and saw "foreigner," "Indian," or "Asian." At that age, it was not obvious to me that I was different from anyone else, because I thought and spoke like an "American." But I didn't look like one to her, which is to say, white. I lived with that tension for years, struggling to figure out where I belonged, seeking to find terms to explain my identity. *What did it mean to be Indian? American? Asian? Brown? What was I? Where did I fit in?*

To make matters more confusing, filling out forms in later years that asked for my race was perplexing. I didn't belong in any category on the list. The closest group was "Asian/Pacific Islander," but that didn't fit because Asia is quite diverse, yet the form only had one box for us all. If a person who didn't know me simply looked at the "Asian/Pacific Islander" box checked on my form, they wouldn't know which country I'm from.

Asians are lumped into one category, one blob, with no distinction made for our unique identities. We don't have a defined country on these forms. We are one mass tied together because of geography. Asia, comprising forty-eight countries, is four times bigger than the United States, and is the most populous continent in the world, with diverse people groups. Yet, Asians are treated as an aggregate. In fact, when I was young, I thought *Asian* referred to someone from China. I didn't realize the term also applied to me!

As a teenager and young adult, I used to be angry at God for my skin color and for putting me in the middle of two cultures. If God wanted me to be Indian, why had my parents left India? If God wanted me to be American, why did I look Indian? Why had God made my life complicated in this way? Everyone had different expectations of me. Americans looked at my external appearance and expected me to be Indian, not knowing if I spoke English. Strangers stayed distant and distrustful because of my skin color, or because of my ethnic name. Indians expected me to be Indian, sometimes speaking to me in Hindi or some other language. Yet I do not speak these languages. I only understand a little bit of my parents' mother tongue, Punjabi. Sometimes I wanted to shout to my peers and the world, "I'm American!"

I went through phases when I rebelled against anything Indian, to the point of saying, "I'm not Indian!" Friends and family would look at me in surprise and amusement because that's not what my skin color conveyed to them. I often felt like I was living in a land of in-between, in a country with no name, a liminal space, not fitting in anywhere.

Other than my own family, I didn't know anyone like myself: of
Indian descent but raised in the United States. Even today, most of
the Indians I know grew up in India and came to the United States
for college or a job. Living in a small southern town, I did not grow
up close to others like me. Plus, most Indians are Hindus, which
placed me further in that land of in-between, for I had broken
with my Hindu background and my parents' religion and began
attending church as a child and teenager.

In my twenties, due to job prospects, I moved from Alabama
to Milwaukee—a city that would later be designated "the most
segregated city in America." People sometimes ask me, "Wasn't it
really racist in the South?" If only racism could be so easily con-
tained. People are often shocked, and some even express disbelief,
when I tell them of my experiences with racism in Milwaukee:
the time when I walked into a store and was ignored while sales-
people approached other customers; being given the finger while
simply driving; the clerk at the exit door at the Costco who spends
extra time looking over my receipt while glossing over others' (I've
counted and watched, multiple times). Or there have been times
when I would share about my experiences and others would launch
into an explanation of the hierarchical structures between Italian,
Polish, German, and other European groups that existed in Milwaukee, and the discrimination against Italians. When I had a
story of oppression to tell, why were white people so quick to draw
parallels with me rather than the oppressor?

People of color have consistently been marginalized in a white-
centric society. We have felt invisible and lonely. We have been
devalued, attacked, beaten, shot, lynched, enslaved, exiled, killed.
Asians have been marginalized and made invisible; Black people
have been devalued, enslaved, and murdered; Indigenous people
have been erased and oppressed; Latin Americans have been

discriminated against and publicly marginalized. This is by no means an exhaustive list of affected groups, and these adjectives are incomplete and inadequate to describe all the trauma, pain, and centuries of oppression. But with increasing loneliness, alienation, disconnection, and polarization not only in the United States but also globally, finding a sense of belonging is an urgent task for the person of color today.

Living in this in-between place lends itself to a peculiar kind of loneliness: specifically, ethnic and racial loneliness. It has taken years to untangle and unpack internal dialogues and assimilation strategies I developed, years of reckoning and soul-searching to reach a place of peace and rest regarding my identity.

There are different kinds of loneliness. Loneliness can be situational, emotional, social, physical, geographic, or spiritual. In this book, I'll focus on racial and ethnic loneliness. This book is about recognizing, living with, and shedding light on this kind of loneliness, and finding hope within it, in spite of it, and beyond it. I'll discuss disbelonging, marginalization, isolation, othering; the longing to belong, to be known, to be seen; and strategies for alleviating ethnic loneliness. Together we'll find out that belonging is multitiered, as we discuss belonging to ourselves, to others, to community, and to God, and it is applicable for those with a faith background or those without. In fact, we might even learn that loneliness is often the status quo rather than the exception, and our places of exile are places we find hope, and where we can find belonging even in spite of living in exile.

I write to honor my parents' experience, other immigrants' experiences, and the experience of people of color. I also write from my own perspective. I cannot pretend to understand the many and varied experiences of all people of color. Yet there are aspects we share, and I hope to shed light on how it feels to be in this liminal space, to remind us that we are not alone. By the end, I hope to help us more deeply understand ethnic and racial loneliness, what can be done to help assuage this ache of loneliness, and how to find a place of belonging.

There is hope for the person of color who feels marginalized and like they are living in in-between spaces. A path toward healing and belonging is possible as we understand and claim our identity. We'll find the answers to that perennial question "So, what are you?" and answers for when we're told to go back to our own individual Indianas, either directly or indirectly. So, let's travel now from this place to that, from a country with no name to new places where we will build a new concept of home, where we feel seen, where we are known, where we belong.

# PART ONE

# SO, WHAT ARE YOU?

*Understanding Ethnic Loneliness*

# 1

# DEFINING ETHNIC LONELINESS

*The most terrible poverty is loneliness,
and the feeling of being unloved.*

MOTHER TERESA

W hat's on the front porch?" I asked, eight years old and inquisitive.

Our family was heading out of the house one sunny morning, and I was the first to step outside. I immediately spotted something unusual in the corner of the porch. It resembled a brown furry animal, but I wasn't sure, so I dashed back indoors and told my parents. They came outside to investigate, thinking it was probably a stray animal.

It turned out to be something very unusual: a dead cat. The cat had been deliberately placed there, and small, metal straight pins had been stuck all over its dead body. Attached to one of the pins was a piece of paper with a message telling my family to leave. My parents ushered my siblings and me indoors and called the police. The police took the corpse away and opened an investigation.

Around the same time this happened, my parents were receiving prank phone calls in the middle of the night. Those were the days before answering machines, caller ID, or smartphones, so my father—a physician who was often on night duty—had to answer the phone in case the hospital was calling. No one spoke on the other end of these prank calls. This went on for days. Calls sometimes came five, six, even seven times per night. My father was losing sleep, and finally he'd had enough. He called the police and reported the prank calls. The police came to our house and put a tap on our phone.

One morning not too long afterward, my father arrived at his office and found the sheriff waiting for him.

"I know who's been calling your place, Doc," the sheriff said.

"Who?" my father asked.

"First, let me ask you if you want to press charges," the sheriff said.

My father told him he couldn't answer that question without knowing who was responsible. When the sheriff told him who the phone taps led to, my father told him not to press charges yet.

"Why do you want to wait?" asked the sheriff.

"Because I know them," my dad replied.

Soon afterward, the sheriff and his deputy paid a visit to the home where the calls had originated. It was a couple, a husband and wife. The police knocked on their door, and the man opened it. He was surprised to see police at the door but let them inside. The officer questioned the man about the prank calls, and the man told the officer he knew nothing about them.

While the officer was questioning the man, the woman walked into the room. At this point, she was aware that the calls had been traced back to their residence. She told the police that someone had broken into their house and used their phone. She said they were frightened by the intrusion and hid in their room while the perpetrator entered their home and used their phone. But what about the fact that the prank calls had happened throughout the night on multiple nights? As incredulous as it was, that was the story they told the police: an intruder had broken into their home several times to use their phone to call our home in the middle of the night. Because of her demeanor and her story, the officer suspected it was she who was making the harassing phone calls.

The officer also noticed something else. The home was filled with cats.

While there was no definitive proof linking this couple to the dead cat on our front porch, it was certainly compelling circumstantial evidence. My father did not prosecute, and the offenders were given a warning. They ended up moving from our town not long afterward, but they never welcomed my family. As it turns out, the man had told my father upon their first introduction to "go back to wherever the hell you came from."

My father had moved our family to this small southern town because the town desperately needed another physician, and my parents liked the southern climate, the picturesque valley in the Appalachian foothills, the schools, and the small-town community. Our family came seeking community and belonging, and while some folks wanted us and were happy to have us there, others were not.

## THE LAND OF LONELINESS

How do you define loneliness? Is it feeling sad? Is it a feeling of isolation? Does the feeling come and go, or persist? Is it possible to be lonely and not depressed? Is solitude a factor, and how is it related to loneliness? How do we measure it, define it, explain it?

Loneliness is a weed, sprouting everywhere we don't want it to be, popping up in the oddest times or during the most usual times in life. We yank it out, and there it is again. We don't know when that lonely ache will pop up. It comes and goes, and while it isn't always on the surface, we live with the expectation that the pain of loneliness will return again and again, exasperating us.

Loneliness is a gentle, persistent rain, a light tapping, never-ending, falling rain amid perpetually gray skies. Or perhaps it is a torrential downpour. We don't know when the rain will stop, when the clouds will shift, when the sun will break through. Perhaps it is a sky with brooding clouds, with ominous weather, thunder and lightning bolts; angry, moody, smoldering.

Loneliness is hunger, coming from a place of ancient and spiritual longing. Loneliness is a howl from a deep space inside of us, crying of division and disconnect from others, ourselves, or God. Loneliness is reminiscent of a hope; a dream, deep and persistent; a desire for authentic connection, community, and belonging. Perhaps it is physical pain. It could be a temporary prick, a jolt, a nonlinear pathway with a trail, somewhat marked, somewhat trod upon. Or perhaps it is a never-ending ache.

Loneliness can feel like any of these, at one time or another, or sometimes several at once. It can be relentless, especially chronic loneliness. The tight claws of chronic loneliness grasp, not letting go, its gnawing teeth biting away at our insides, chewing away our sense of place, belonging, and identity. Loneliness is a land without borders. It can affect anyone.

Loneliness is an Immigrant. Loneliness is Foreigner. Loneliness is Other, Unknown, Unseen, Forgotten, Invisible, Misunderstood, Excluded, Enslaved, Displaced, Last, Unwanted. Assimilated. Unassimilated. Segregated. Desegregated. Attacked. Hated. Lynched. Murdered.

Loneliness is a refugee, third culture kid, transracial adoptee. It is someone who is biracial, multiracial, living in the thin space between two or more cultures or ethnicities.

Maybe this ache sounds familiar and such a sense or feeling has come and gone for you, like an ebb and flow, or perhaps it feels like a constant weight. Think of the people you know. What faces come to your mind when you think of loneliness?[1]

Loneliness is complicated to define. Is loneliness an emotion, a psychological condition, or a physical and emotional state? Fay Bound Alberti, in *A Biography of Loneliness*, describes it as an "emotion cluster, a blend of different emotions," such as sorrow, grief, and anger, because no single emotion adequately sums up the condition.[2] We can break loneliness further into more specific types: relational loneliness, geographic loneliness, ethical loneliness, spiritual loneliness, and ethnic and racial loneliness. We could have one or some combination of these. Each possesses its own cluster of emotional and physiological responses, manifests in us differently, impacts every aspect of our being (physical, emotional, social, spiritual), and is dependent on our geographical location, our time in history, our social location, and our social connection.[3]

In his book *Together*, Surgeon General of the United States Vivek H. Murthy considers loneliness of utmost public health importance, describing it as "the subjective feeling that you're lacking the social connections you need."[4] Loneliness affects mental health, physical health, and all dimensions of our well-being. One study reports that loneliness reduces lifespan as much as smoking fifteen cigarettes a day,[5] and increases the risk of premature death by 26 percent.[6] An experiment conducted at UCLA found loneliness affects the brain in a similar way as physical pain.[7] Moreover, the Framingham Heart study documented that loneliness occurs in clusters and is, in fact, contagious.[8] A survey in 2021 reported that Americans have fewer friends than ever before, with 12 percent saying they have no friends at all, and 40 percent saying they have no "best friend."[9] A Harvard report corroborates this fact, finding that 36 percent of Americans feel lonely frequently or almost all of the time.[10]

Murthy released an advisory report in 2023, reiterating the urgent public health matter of *social connection*. Social connection is defined as the size and diversity of one's social network and the roles the relationships serve in our networks—and the report found we're severely lacking it. A lack of social connection is associated with an increased risk of heart disease, stroke, depression, anxiety, and dementia. In fact, social connection is a *social determinant of health*, in addition to community well-being, community resilience and safety, and economic prosperity. Social connection is, in fact, "a fundamental need, as essential to survival as food, water, and shelter."[11] With these kinds of statistics, we can be certain that some of the people we encounter every day are lonely; in fact, it might even be us.

There are significant economic costs to loneliness, which is probably one reason the United Kingdom and Japan both have ministers of loneliness: the health and social needs of the lonely cost money, and those needs are increasing in the West as the population ages.[12] Social isolation is responsible for $6.7 billion in Medicare costs for older adults. In fact, a Dutch grocery chain added checkout lanes specifically for the elderly, where customers can take their time and chat with cashiers—called the "chat checkout"—designed to help with loneliness. A Canadian supermarket implemented the same concept, and Americans have called on Walmart and Kroger to do the same, instead of building more self-checkout lanes.[13]

Although loneliness is an epidemic of wide proportions, no official "diagnosis" exists for loneliness: there is no test, x-ray, treatment, or diagnostic code for loneliness. We recognize and define depression, anxiety, and other mental health conditions, but not loneliness—although it is a major public health concern reaching beyond other prevalent physical conditions such as diabetes or obesity.

We have no official diagnosis, nor do we have a pill to cure the pang of loneliness. But we know this much: the solution includes tender human touches of social connection and knowing who and whose we are, and we know loneliness is connected to belonging. But specifically, how do we define ethnic loneliness?

## WHAT IS ETHNIC LONELINESS?

A good friend of mine suffers from an undefined chronic illness. She has visited doctor after doctor, sharing her symptoms with specialists for years with no answers. Test after test turns up negative, but she still experiences physical symptoms that current medical technology cannot account for. Because her tests are negative, her symptoms are dismissed or ignored, or she's told it's "depression." Sometimes *depression* is used as a catchall for what cannot be explained, and it's a term often dispensed to women.

Little consideration is given to the idea that we haven't yet developed tests to adequately recognize or name each and every ailment. Our tests are simply tools available at this time in the history of medical and technological development. So, my friend slips in and out of medical offices and in the enigmatic space of having an unexplained illness, with no abatement of symptoms; a plethora of questions, tests, treatments; thousands of dollars spent, as well as tears; but distressingly no answers.

Like those with chronic illnesses attempting to explain their conditions, ethnic and racial minority groups have been explaining our situation and experiences, too. Ethnic loneliness is a condition that also has no official diagnosis and is a term not yet fully defined. The illness people of color are trying to explain is the loneliness of being disenfranchised, excluded, invisible, othered, marginalized, isolated, unseen, attacked, hated. Like the patient with the unexplained chronic illness, minority groups also encounter the roadblocks of having our experiences dismissed as nonexistent or minimized. This book seeks to define and name that experience.

Ethnic loneliness occurs when we feel disconnected or culturally isolated as a result of our racial or ethnic identity. We can experience any of the following:

- *Cultural isolation*: when we are surrounded by those who do not share our cultural background, traditions, and perspectives
- *Lack of connection*: when we are unable to relate to others around us due to cultural differences
- *Identity conflicts*: when we struggle with our sense of identity, and feel torn between our ethnic or cultural heritage and the need to conform to the dominant culture
- *Loss of cultural identity*: when we distance ourselves from our own cultures to fit with majority culture
- *Social exclusion*: when we are excluded from social activities or conversations due to cultural differences
- *Marginalization*: when we encounter social, economic, or political challenges as a result of smaller numbers or cultural norms
- *Language barriers*: when we have our own languages or ways of communication that are different from the dominant culture and seek to preserve this element of our cultural identity
- *Integration and assimilation*: when we attempt to balance preserving our cultural heritage and assimilating in broader society, which can lead to us navigating multiple identities

Cultural isolation and the above situations can have far-reaching effects on mental health. When we are disconnected from our cultural heritage and ethnic identities, it can lead to depression, anxiety, low self-esteem, stress, an identity crisis, alienation, and loneliness.

Factors in our environment, our genetics, our immune systems, the geographic areas we live in, and the infrastructure of our cities all affect ethnic loneliness. Health care policies, food access, use of technology, family structure, physical safety, present and generational trauma, and poverty all affect our sense of belonging and loneliness. Even as I share about loneliness, I recognize I share from a place of some privilege. My father was a physician, and I didn't grow up with financial or food insecurity, another dimension of privilege.

To be ethnically lonely means the scars are a result of not only racial constructs and systems in society but also various cultural differences and values that are in tension between the ethnic minority's culture and culture at-large. Such specific cultural differences include:

- varying views on success
- conflicting educational and career expectations
- clashing values regarding honoring the family and/or parents of origin or following the culture
- differences in language and worldview
- generational differences with older versus younger generations
- individualist versus collectivist values
- differentials in viewing authority figures

In addition, loneliness is compounded when the majority culture offers solutions to ethnic minorities that are insensitive to our differences. Such solutions include "Assimilate and erase your ethnic and racial identity as much as possible and conform to white normative standards." "Be like us." "Let go of your culture, your background." "Ignore your family and what they want." "Straighten your hair." "Change your accent." "Change your name." "Don't listen to your family."

On an anonymous, qualitative survey on ethnicity and belonging I conducted with over forty-five respondents, an Asian American respondent who attended a predominantly white university explained she worked so hard to assimilate that white friends would tell her, "Wow, I really don't see you as Asian." She wrote that she initially internalized this as a positive thing but realized it isolated her from other minority students.

A respondent who identified as Black and of African descent wrote, "Growing up as a kid, I never saw anyone who looked like me at school, in books, or in movies, and no one had ever heard of Eritrea, where my family is from. I felt alienated at hair salons, at school, in drama club, in friend groups, at clothing stores, at the masjid."

Meghan O'Rourke, editor of the *Yale Review*, writes of her years of living with a chronic illness in *The Invisible Kingdom*: "It took years before I realized that the illness was not just my own; the silence around suffering was our society's pathology."[14] In the case of ethnic and racial loneliness, the silence and denial of systemic and institutional realities that perpetuate loneliness and "othering" is also our society's pathology. When the process of ethnic identity formation is disrupted or denigrated, the result is disillusionment, fear, confusion, grief, alienation, frustration, anger, and loneliness. Brown, Black, Asian, Latin American, Indigenous, Mixed race, and other minority ethnic and racial groups long for recognition of this reality.

## DEFINING TERMS

In understanding ethnic loneliness, it's helpful to first start with a few definitions: *POC, BIPOC, Brown, whiteness, ethnicity,* and *race,* as well as *Hispanic, Latino,* and *Latin American; AAPI* and *Asian American;* and *Black, African American,* and *African descent.*

Globally, three-quarters of the world's population live in Asia or Africa and is likely categorized as a *person of color.*[15] With the global majority of humans as people of color, this term *person of color (POC)* arises from the perspective of the white majority, or rather, from the perspective of who is in power and who defines it as such. If people of color had been in charge of the defining, we must wonder if that term would be in our current lexicon.

The term *people of color* first appeared in the United States in the 1700s and was meant as a category for nonwhites, and then re-emerged in the 1970s. The term now encompasses Hispanics, Asians, Native Americans, and Black people. Some feel, however, the term *POC* doesn't adequately address the fact "that certain effects of racism—mass incarceration, police violence, inability to access good health care—disproportionately affect Black and Indigenous people."[16] A friend of mine of African descent objects to the term because it has its roots in enslavement and centers the perspective of the white oppressor, though she acknowledges she is in the minority opinion among other Black folks on this. I've come across Asians and Indian Americans who do not consider themselves a "person of color." And while a panethnic term like *BIPOC* (Black, Indigenous, and People of Color) serves as a term of collective organization and generalizes the experiences of ethnic minorities, it also flattens identities and differences among our various ethnic and racial groups.[17] For the purposes of this book, we use the term *BIPOC* to address the common experiences of marginalization of minority groups, while acknowledging that our terms have limitations, and all experiences cannot be distilled into a single one that speaks for all.

*Brown*, also, is more than just an adjective for many cultural and ethnic groups. Dr. Robert Chao Romero, professor of Chicana/o and Asian American studies at UCLA, explains *Brown* is also a process, as certain ethnic groups have transitioned from Brown to whiteness, such as Italians, Greeks, Ashkenazi Jews, and other groups who used to occupy the space of Brown. For example, he explains Brown as a "liminal, social, legal, political, and cultural space" the Latin American community has inhabited since the US-Mexico War and the Treaty of Guadalupe-Hidalgo of 1848. And even though during the era of Jim Crow Latin Americans were legally considered white, they were still segregated and treated unequally through legal loopholes and social conventions.[18]

In addition, *whiteness* is not a person of European descent but "a way of being in the world and seeing the world that forms cognitive and affectional structures able to seduce people into its habitation and meaning making" according to Dr. Willie James Jennings, associate professor of systematic theology and Africana studies at Yale.[19] The Smithsonian National Museum of African American History & Culture defines whiteness this way:

> *Whiteness* and white racialized identity refer to the way that white people and their customs, culture, and beliefs operate as the standard by which all other groups are compared. Whiteness is also at the core of understanding race in America. Whiteness and the normalization of white racial identity throughout America's history have created a culture where nonwhite persons are seen as inferior or abnormal.
>
> This white-dominant culture also operates as a social mechanism that grants advantages to white people, since they can navigate society both by feeling normal and being viewed as normal. Persons who identify as white rarely have to think about their racial identity because they live within a culture where whiteness has been normalized.[20]

*Race* is a classification of people according to their physical traits and ancestry. It is a social construct. One's race is not always obvious or evident, yet it is a construct with tangible consequences. Some constructs can actually help us understand human experiences and build bridges, whereas others divide and damage. The construction of race falls in the latter category, as it has been used as a means of power and subjugation.

*Ethnicity*, as adapted from *Beyond Colorblind* by Sarah Shin, speaker and trainer in ethnicity, is more distinct and specific than race, referring to a common ancestry, tribe, nationality, background, and typically with shared customs, language, values, traditions, religious practices, and history.[21] While we can see food, language, clothing, and traditions, we cannot see under the surface to deeper values such as one's relationship with authority; values regarding family, marriage, and children; notions of justice and fairness; roles regarding age and gender; rules and expectations; communication styles; power dynamics; how conflict is handled; and customs and beliefs about hospitality.

*Hispanic* generally refers to people who speak Spanish or are descended from Spanish speakers. The term came into use during Nixon's presidency (1968–1974) and appeared on the census in 1980. Since *Hispanic* refers to language, it is an element of culture and more closely associated with ethnicity than race. Moreover, people of all races identify as Hispanic, and today, people can select other racial categories along with Hispanic, such as white, Black, Asian, American Indian, Pacific Islander, or some other race, on census forms.[22] Yet, there is also a sense of colonialization and loss attached with the term *Hispanic*, so some Latinos avoid that term.[23]

*Latino* is a term that refers to geography, generally meaning people who are from Latin America. *Latino* does not technically refer to race either. Anyone from Central or South America and the Caribbean can be described as Latino. Within this group, there are varieties of races. Latinos can be white, Black, Mixed, Indigenous, or even of Asian descent.[24] In this book, I use the terms *Hispanic*, *Latino*, and *Latin American* according to how a particular survey or original source categorized the term. But it's important to recognize the heterogeneity of this group, representing twenty different countries and territories.

The term *Asian American* was conceived in the 1960s by activists to bring together the Asian community.[25] The term is everywhere now, but it's a sweeping term that also has its limitations. It erases the unique heritages and cultural differences among Asians and minimizes specific cultural and community needs. While it has been helpful politically, individual ethnicities and marginalized Asian American groups are not all recognized equally. In the 1980s and 1990s, the term was broadened to *AAPI* (Asian American and Pacific Islander), which has helped to unify the experiences of Asians, but the term is still quite broad and erases groups.[26] The term *Asian American* (or *AAPI*) is used in this book, while recognizing its limits.

The term *African American* was promoted in 1988 by the Rev. Jesse Jackson, and it gained popularity.[27] But some feel that the term *Black* actually is better, because it celebrates race and culture from all over the world.[28] Both terms *Black* and *African American* are commonly used today, but these also have limitations and are not, in fact, interchangeable. While many African Americans do have African ancestry, the term does not include those from the Caribbean or Europe.[29] A Gallup poll conducted in 2019 asked which term was preferred, *Black* or *African American*, and the dominant response was "it does not matter." Other polls conducted without the "it does not matter option" found Black Americans split, with a slight edge of 42 percent preferring *Black*, 35 percent preferring *African American*, 7 percent saying they preferred another term, and 13 percent saying it doesn't make a difference.[30]

In 2020, the Associated Press (and other news organizations), began capitalizing *Black*, which caused some debate. The choice to capitalize *Black* refers to the fact that being Black shapes the core identity of a Black person in the United States. Not all African Americans agree with the capitalization, however, because it lumps all of the African diaspora into a monolithic group and erases the diversity of all the different groups.[31] I follow the news reporting conventions of capitalizing Black, and I utilize both *Black* and *African American* as terms in these pages.

One thing is clear with the labels: they are imperfect. There isn't a clear consensus on how to identify our unique differences but it's important we recognize the nuances, strengths, and weaknesses of each term. Within each of these labels of *Latino* or *Hispanic*, *Asian American*, *Black* or *African American* are hundreds of ethnic groups with distinct cultures and languages and differences, coupled with histories and meanings and multiple perspectives. Our terms are inadequate, and our language usage is still evolving.

## SO, WHAT ARE YOU?

If you ask me what I am, I could tell you I was born in India, grew up in the southern United States, and then moved to the upper Midwest in my twenties. But even that wouldn't tell you who I *really* am. That basic information doesn't inform you that I am *Punjabi*. Folks from India identify ourselves according to which Indian state we're from (Punjab in my case) and what language we speak (or our family speaks). To tell you I'm "Indian" isn't truly adequate for you to know "what I am." Punjabis are known for the Bhangra dance, which is a traditional folk dance that originated with Sikh and Muslim farmers in villages and rural areas. It was performed while farmers were doing their agricultural chores, with some of the dance moves having roots in farming activities.[32] Today, Bhangra is also a form of music and song. To know Punjabis is to know and understand Bhangra and its importance in culture.

But to tell you I'm Punjabi isn't adequate either, because in modern India, the state of Punjab is largely composed of two major religions: Hindu and Sikh. Among other Indians, I often have to distinguish myself as from a Punjabi Hindu family, because that is my family's identity. Each state in India has its own unique customs, language, food, and traditions. To be from a particular state in India means something; India is not a monolith—just as someone born and raised in the Bronx has had a completely different upbringing from someone raised in Iowa or in Southern California.

It's also important to know that my family has our own stories of experiencing the Partition of India in 1947, which was the largest mass migration at that time in history, with at least fourteen million displaced people moving between Pakistan and India, when the country was suddenly divided. Many families from India have their own Partition stories to tell. My father, who grew up in a village not far from the border of Pakistan, was a young boy during Partition. He remembers carrying stacks of hot *rotis* (flatbread) and *sabzis* (vegetable curries) to those fleeing from Pakistan and migrating to India. Families spent days cooking and making meals for refugees, taking them to the border, to the train station, and handing out food to fatigued travelers who left in a hurry, walking on foot, with only what they could carry on their backs.

My mother grew up in that same village. Her grandparents and family crossed the border from Pakistan to India along with my mother's aunt Prem, who was a teenager at the time, and who became seriously ill during the journey. The journey took several months. It was horrific. People were kidnapped, slaughtered, raped—and some of them by their own friends and neighbors. The entire history of the Partition is itself its own complex book. Yet, you wouldn't necessarily know that this is part of my story, just by the question of "So what are you?" You wouldn't know the history and generational trauma I carry in my experience and body.

You also wouldn't know I attended a church in a small town in Alabama, and how strange that must have been for my parents.

There was no other option. While my counterparts (Indian teens) who lived in places heavily populated by Indians, such as New York or Fremont, California, were going to the Hindu temple on Sundays for language and culture studies, I was attending church in rural Alabama. Of course, my parents were the ones who first took us to church, but it was even stranger to them, I suppose, that eventually I asked to keep going.

To be asked these questions, "So what are you? Where are you from? No, where are you *really* from?" automatically sets a line between people of color and white folks about how we are different, suggesting an attempt to distance us from them and keep us labeled as "other." There are occasions when a person is genuinely interested and cares, and there are also instances when these questions actually mean, "I'm not sure if I can trust you," and, "You look different, and different isn't good." The questions are asking us to define ourselves at that instant, so others can make a quick judgment on our answers. In the context of friendship, we share our values, beliefs, and ideas over time and shared conversation. But without the context of relationship, these types of questions can be used to make assumptions and conclusions, and are a shortcut to comfort. I have people judging me continuously as a woman and based on the color of my skin. Whatever narratives others have, I'm lumped in there without having a chance, without them getting to know me. It's lonely in here.

## A PECULIAR ALONENESS

In the biblical story of creation when Adam is naming the animals and creatures all around him, he realizes that he is the only one of his particular *kind*—that is, human. He doesn't have a counterpart to share and delight in the beauty of the world around him. No one else to banter with, to discuss the naming of the creatures. Though he walks with God, it is a peculiar kind of aloneness, and God says it is not good for him to be alone, so God makes a companion, a friend, one of his "kind." God creates Eve.

When Adam and Eve eat the forbidden fruit and are banished from the Garden, they experience separation and the loneliness of being apart from God. There is no way to return to that idyllic paradise. Angels keep guard over Eden, not allowing passage back inside. We can imagine the profound grief and loneliness Adam and Eve experienced at that separation. In a sense, we continue to experience that peculiar aloneness today because we, too, are banished from the Garden, as humankind longs for spiritual reconciliation with our Creator. History is replete with stories and legends of the human desire for a fountain of youth, an ancient longing for the immortality and mystery of Eden and reconciliation with God.

Just as we live in exile from Eden, we find ourselves also living in degrees of exile, or separation, from one another. Feelings of disbelonging exist on a continuum, and we all experience them in some capacity. For the ethnic and racial minority in white-majority spaces, though, these feelings are an everyday experience.

I never heard my parents speak ill of those people who harassed us. It is now part of family lore and legend. It's a story of courage and resilience because it was frightening to receive such a hateful message and still resolve to stay. I wonder, *Would I be so bold myself if it happened to me today? Would such an occurrence be considered a hate crime today and result in an additional charge for cruelty to animals?* People didn't know my family, or other Indian American folks, when we first showed up in our small Alabama town. We tend to fear what we don't know. Fear leads to hatred, and hatred leads to violence, which leads to things like dead cats flung on porches.

There is an ancient Jewish story of a rabbi and his disciple that goes something like this:

Disciple to Rabbi: "I love you."

Rabbi: "Do you know what hurts me?"

Disciple: "You're confusing me with irrelevant questions. I don't understand."

Rabbi: "Do you know what hurts me? My question is not strange or irrelevant. It is the soul of understanding love and compassion. For if you do not know what hurts, how can you truly love me?"[33]

Do we know what hurts the people around us, especially those who do not look like us? Are we asking, yearning to know this from each other? It's a deep question. Might we ask one another, "What brings you joy?" or "What hurts you?" instead of "What are you?"? We would learn "what" we truly are more quickly by speaking of matters of the heart and soul.

People of color are doing what we must to survive. In many cases, assimilating and letting go of their own culture was the only option for our parents and relatives—but is it the same for us? As increased mobility and demographics change the composition of the United States, it is urgent that we help the ethnic minority find a sense of belonging and live wholly and fully amid the wilds of loneliness.

The country we are imagining is one in which we all belong. As we embark on this journey to a better country, we'll talk about how to find belonging to ourselves, to others, to our communities, and to God. We'll find that our lands of loneliness are pathways to beauty and wholeness. Our desire for a new country can be a doorway to light, a passageway to a Spacious and Beautiful Land we didn't know existed.

## SO, WHAT ARE YOU?

You belong
In your skin
Your ethnicity
Your culture
And your "kind"
Is good
And wanted
And needed
What hurts you
Hurts me, hurts us all
On the island of disbelonging
You are rich in love
By others
Who want to love you
The universe
Opens its arms to you

## QUESTIONS FOR REFLECTION
## AND DISCUSSION

1. What is your ethnic, racial, and cultural background? How
   do you identify yourself? Be as detailed as possible.
2. Writing prompts:
   • "Something I appreciate about my ethnic background
     is . . ."
   • "Something I appreciate about my family's culture is . . ."
3. What is your experience of ethnic loneliness? What else
   would you add to the definition?

# 2

# DISBELONGING AND HOME

*Do you understand the sadness of geography?*

MICHAEL ONDAATJE

Not too long ago, I found myself wandering the grounds of a college campus that had a monastery. I had never been to a monastery, so monks strolling around in long brown capes was an unusual sight. While there, I learned that Benedictine monks take several vows, including a vow of stability. In other words, they vow to stay put. They won't move every three years, search for a better monastery, or drift from one place to another. They vow to stay in the same place as long as they live.

As someone who has had the identity of being an immigrant all of my life, this vow feels foreign to me. Even though my parents stayed in the same house in the United States for forty-five years, I can't imagine making such a vow, because I'm nagged by questions: *Will I not need to go from one place to another at some point? How could I live with such a resoluteness to never leave one place, because how could I know the future?* I feel the tension between wanting to stay, grow roots, and develop relationships, and simultaneously wondering about life elsewhere, knowing circumstances may require me to make a change. And yet there are monks who make a solemn decision to *belong* to that one place, to stay, to grow roots.

The way of monks is, I confess, a mystery to me, and I find this vow of stability both admirable and frightening.

## SWEET (AND SPICY) HOME ALABAMA

When my family moved to Alabama, my parents bought their first house. I remember looking at houses as a child with my parents and being in awe. All the houses seemed magical—they were full of many windows and had carpeting with dust motes floating in the air like fairy dust. When my parents asked me what I liked, I said I liked everything, because I did.

My parents chose a two-story blond-brick house on the edge of town, near the hospital where my father worked, and a ten-minute drive to school. It amuses me that we called it "blond brick." I thought it was the color of vanilla pudding. We were the Brown family living in the blond-brick house.

We sold that childhood home in 2022. It was the season to downsize, but the process was heartbreaking nonetheless. My mother said that moving from there felt the same as when she left India for America. She and my father lived in that one house for forty-five years—longer than they lived in India. It was *home*. The tiny galley kitchen, the screened-in porch with the swing that I greatly miss—all became home.

I thought my parents would stay in that home forever. I thought I'd have more years to sit in the formal living room with the lace curtains and the china cabinet and the sofa with the orange flowers, out of date as it is now, but somehow fitting in that room, looking as if it belonged there. I recall sitting in the 1970s gold-striped upholstered swivel chairs, surveying the beauty of the room. The walls and tables were covered with family photos, and the room was adorned with a few beautiful keepsakes from India, like a tall brass lamp and mirrored elephant figurines. That was the "company room." When I was a child, it was off-limits.

I didn't have a TV in my room or the latest gadgets like my peers, but we had an Atari (the grandfather of modern video games!), a Barbie townhouse, Monopoly, and an upright piano. I could skateboard halfway down our long sloping driveway without falling and had enough scraped knees to show how much practice it required to achieve that feat. I think I might have been the first Indian immigrant to skateboard or roller skate on that street in that little town.

Soon after we had moved into that house, with the encouragement of my parents, I invited a friend over after school and to stay for dinner. My parents made hamburgers (and my mother doesn't even eat beef). My friend later told me that her mother had told her she wasn't sure what food we'd serve, but to be polite and say "yes, ma'am," or "no, thank you, ma'am." Southerners are taught gracious manners. My friend liked the hamburgers my parents made, which were flavorful and seasoned with spices, and had grated vegetables and other ingredients all thrown in and cooked. My father likes to remind me that the reason they dumped all those vegetables in was because I started to balk at eating Indian food. I wanted to eat burgers, pizza, and hot dogs like everyone else. The school cafeteria didn't serve vegetable curries. So, my parents started adding vegetables to our burgers, and well, if they aren't the best burgers I've ever eaten. My friend went home with the news of how good the burgers were and to this day, that is how I make my burgers too.

After my siblings and I moved away and had kids of our own, my mother was always ready for us whenever we had a chance to visit. She had books, games, and homemade chicken nuggets (instead of burgers) waiting for us. If it had been India, relatives would have come and gone frequently from the house. "Nobody was alone," my mother once told me, when she shared stories about her growing up years. But in this small southern town in the United States, it was just us, without relatives coming and going. Most of the time it was just us, too, on holidays, though we did have a close American friend whom we called "Grandma Sue," who sometimes joined us (or we joined her).

When my mother was young, I'm sure she never imagined she'd live in a country far away, start a new home, and see her family of origin only a few times afterward. I am sure she never imagined she'd live in a two-story blond-brick house in a small town in Alabama, and that would become her longest geographic home.

Our home in Alabama was the permanent place in my mind, the home where I imagined this branch of our family would congregate. This place is where my life felt rooted, even if I can't imagine a monk's vow to simply stay. (A lot of us can't imagine this anymore. Nowadays, a person in the United States is expected to move eleven times during their lifetime.[1]) Immigrants and displaced persons carry all kinds of images of home in their heads. For my parents, it was their home in India and that Alabama home. For me it was that Alabama home, too, as complex as the history and memories might be. Some dreams will live on in new ways.

## A TRIP TO INDIA

When I was in third grade, our family visited India. India was (and is) a feast for all five senses. In my parents' village, open sewers lined the edges of the streets, and we children were warned not to play there. Cows and other animals roamed freely, sharing narrow spaces with rickshaws, bicycles, pedestrians, and cars.

We visited a farm owned by my maternal grandfather, where he grew crops such as wheat, cotton, sugar cane, carrots, and potatoes.

We watched buffalo yoked to a rod that stirred and cooked the sugar cane. We chewed on raw sugar cane stalks, the sugary goodness tickling our tongues. When my mother was young, going to the farm was a special event. It was special for me too. I had my first Hindi lessons there, and I still remember the first words I learned: *hathi* means "elephant," and *billi* means "cat."

I was awestruck by India. Never in my life had I seen such a place. It was a world apart from the snow-laden streets of South Dakota, and the lush green hills of our Alabama town, and our yard of Bermuda grass dotted with pink azalea bushes. In India, my nose was assaulted with the aromas of both the sewers and the spices of good foods, the smell of old-fashioned ink pens and my little notebook, the waft of cow dung, and the choking air of smoke belching from diesel lorries.

I marveled at the toilets. Actually, it would be more accurate to say I was frustrated with them. No, truthfully, I hated the toilets. They were essentially holes in the ground. In lieu of toilet paper, there was a water spigot and a small plastic bucket with a handle. It was all so strange to my eight-year-old self. I hadn't yet been told to go back to where I came from (that was still to come), but I didn't want to be from this distant place with the "squatty potties."

When I returned to the United States, my head was full of stories of the newness, the excitement. I wanted to tell *someone* about the sewers, the cows roaming freely, the odors, the dust, and the heat. I wanted to share how much I hated those toilets, how sweet the sugar cane was, and the new words I learned. I wanted to say, "Hey, did you know there's a country on the other side of the world where it's like this? Where you can't sit on a toilet because they don't have toilets with seats? Where you can chew on a sugar cane stalk straight from the ground? Where my grandfather rides a horse on his farm? Where they cook flatbread in an

oval-shaped hollow clay oven in the kitchen? Where the houses
are square, with an open courtyard in the middle and rooms off
to the sides? Where they have flat rooftops that look like decks,
and one house may have several? Have you ever seen a house with
multiple flat rooftops, and slept outdoors on a cot under the stars?
Do you know where I have been and the things I have witnessed
and seen, and did you know that there is a whole world out there
that is vastly different from this one, the small town in Alabama
where we live?" But there was no one to talk to. We had just moved
to a small town in Alabama from an even smaller town in South
Dakota, and I hardly knew anyone. These stories were bursting
with nowhere to go.

## DREAMS FIND A PLACE TO LAND

When my parents were still living in India, my father would go
to the rooftop and listen to BBC radio. One day he heard about
a writing contest in Hindi, and so my mom entered. She used to
write stories that were printed in a local Hindi newspaper, as well
as for her college paper. One day, just before immigrating to America,
my father was on the rooftop listening to the radio and heard this:
*Chander Verma of Fazilka, India,* had won first place in an essay
contest. The topic was "What are three things you will teach your
children to be successful in life?" My mother's three things were
self-control, self-dependence, and self-confidence. My parents
planned on stopping in London on their way while immigrating
to America to personally pick up the award, but alas, they didn't
have time to leave the airport during their layover. Perhaps the
award is still gathering dust on some shelf in the BBC's basement.

That unclaimed award has remained a source of pride for years,
a story my mother carries, which I now carry. My mother recited
poems at my brother's wedding and a friend's wedding, and I like

to think some of her writing genes are inscribed in my own DNA. Does the universe have a way of fulfilling the previous generations' past dreams and desires? The way longings search for fulfillment through generations is a mystery. Instead of only generational trauma, we also pass down dreams (and blessings). I think this is part of my story too.

I miss sitting, daydreaming, thinking, or napping on the swing on the back-screened deck of that Alabama home the most, listening to the rain pitter-patter quietly all around me, the pines swaying in the breeze, the birds twittering about. My memories are sealed in those walls, our tears and dreams buried in its hearth, and some have flown away in the wind. The hard and beautiful coexist in my memory. I feel as if I carry my parents' immigrant dreams as well as those of my own, making my way in this land. I can't predict much of anything, except for turns and potholes and bends and thickets. We hold one set of dreams, and life hands us another.

## THE MOST IMPORTANT LEGISLATION NO ONE'S EVER HEARD OF

A single piece of legislation, more than any other, is responsible for changing the demographic landscape of America into the way we know it today, and it is what opened the door for my parents to come to the United States: the Immigration and Nationality Act of 1965. At the time of the passage of the Immigration Act, Lyndon B. Johnson remarked, "This bill that we sign today is not a revolutionary bill. It does not affect the lives of millions. It will not reshape the structure of our daily lives."[2] But either he was mistaken or was downplaying its significance, because this act would dramatically alter the demographic landscape of the United States. In fact, the Immigration Act of 1965 has been called the "most important piece of legislation that no one's ever heard of."[3]

Because of this act, as of 2018, nearly forty-five million immigrants have come to the United States since 1965, significantly altering the configuration of the population of the United States. This number of immigrants is projected to reach seventy-eight million by 2065.[4] *Nothing else* has single-handedly changed the entire demographic composition of the United States more than immigration. As of 2021, the United States population is 59 percent white, 19 percent Hispanic/Latino, 12.6 percent Black, 6 percent Asian, 2.3 percent multiracial, 0.7 percent American Indian/Alaska Native, and 0.2 percent Native Hawaiian and other Pacific Islander.[5] Because of this legislation, the United States will have a nonwhite majority population (all races combined) by the year 2045.[6]

It was the civil rights movement and the Civil Rights Act of 1964 that paved the way for the passage of the Immigration and Nationality Act of 1965. Immigration reform was actually considered part of the civil rights movement, as it was an act that sought to address racial discrimination in immigration policy. Many of us immigrants can thank the civil rights efforts, which paved the way for us to come to the United States.[7]

My father, an Indian-trained physician, still has a copy of the letter that granted him a spot for residency training at a New Jersey hospital. Though he had already been licensed and trained in India, he was required to repeat the residency training process. The United States was in need of physicians and welcomed him in 1969, after the passage of the Immigration Act. In fact, many of the early immigrants either were related to someone already in the United States or had special skills or academic knowledge.

## DEMOGRAPHIC CHANGES AHEAD

A population changes in three different ways: births, deaths, and migration. When births are greater than deaths, it is called a natural increase in population. Conversely, if deaths are greater than births, it is called a natural decrease in population. Migration refers to the movement of people in and out of a country. The next few decades will be demographic turning points in the United States:

- By 2030, baby boomers will be over sixty-five years of age, which means one out of five Americans is projected to be at retirement age.[8]
- By 2030, immigration is projected to overtake natural increase as the *primary* driver for population growth.[9]
- The population of people who are two or more races is projected to be the fastest-growing racial or ethnic group over the next several decades, followed by Asians and Hispanics.[10]
- International migration is simultaneously adding to the population and contributing to the increase in diversity. In recent years, the level of international migration from Mexico has decreased while migration from India and China has increased.[11]
- Asians were the fastest-growing ethnic group in the United States from 2000 to 2019, and by 2060, are expected to triple their 2000 population, rising to 35.8 million. Hispanics were the second fastest-growing group in that same time period.[12]
- The Hispanic population is expected to reach 111 million by 2060.[13]

These are major changes. They demand we consider an array of infrastructural issues and services that will be required to meet the needs of an aging and immigrant population. What is the impact of all these demographic changes on ethnic loneliness?

- The United States will become even more culturally diverse, with more languages, traditions, and customs.
- Political power dynamics could shift as minority or nonwhite populations grow in number and representation.

- A diverse workforce could contribute to innovation and economic growth through a variety of perspectives and skills.
- The educational system will need to adapt to serve the needs of diverse students, including awareness of cultural sensitivity.
- A majority nonwhite population could foster a more global perspective, reflecting the interconnectedness of cultures and nations.
- A more diverse population might lead to discussions about multilingualism and cultural competency—and a greater need for these skills.
- Policy priorities in areas of healthcare, social services, and education might shift to address the unique needs of a changing demographic.

Just because statistically the numbers are going to tip in the direction of a nonwhite majority, however, doesn't mean we will automatically observe discernible representative change around us. It doesn't necessarily mean there will be, for example, four Indian students in an elementary school like the one I attended in Alabama instead of two. It doesn't mean that Congress will automatically have 51 percent nonwhite members, or we'll have a majority of nonwhite CEOs. It means that the numbers themselves will tip past 50 percent nonwhite, but systems, structures, pathways, and inroads to jobs and opportunities—and belonging—aren't going to automatically open. In fact, to use the terms *majority* and *minority* as simply representative in terms of numbers is missing the point.

Adrian Pei, in *The Minority Experience*, defines *minority* and *majority* as who has the "power."[14] *Power* is defined as "not having to think about something that is significant to somebody else."[15] Whoever holds the power is the majority culture. In the case of the United States, numbers by themselves do not automatically translate into a change of power dynamics. There is still work to do in terms of redesigning power and societal structures and institutional systems. And, in fact, the global majority is nonwhite, yet the power exists globally with white populations.

Sadly, sometimes those who pride themselves on being neighborly are the most resistant to America's demographic change. If we consider the views of different religious groups in the United States, we learn that "the majority of Americans in every demographic support welcoming refugees (a different legal classification from immigrants)—into the United States—*except* for white evangelical Christians. Instead, the majority of white evangelicals favor preventing refugee resettlement in the USA."[16] Further, "nearly half of evangelicals saw recent immigrants as an undesirable drain on economic resources." One might think those in the church would be leading the charge to love their neighbor across lines of difference, as Christians are exhorted to love the foreigners among them—yet the reality is some are, and some are not.

## "HOMELESSNESS" AND MULTIGENERATIONAL HOUSEHOLDS

Though it wasn't always easy to live in the Deep South, and though we all have our own difficult and happy memories, our home was *ours*. It was a tangible piece of our American dream. My dad had work, and we had a house. My parents had created something from a twenty-dollar bill. It was all more than they could have ever imagined or believed, coming from a tiny village in India that no one had heard of.

In *A Biography of Loneliness*, Alberti writes that loneliness is also felt among those who feel "rootless" (not just roofless).[17] Loneliness is actually a lack of physical safety and "social belonging."[18] Natasha Sistrunk Robinson writes of this sense in *A Sojourner's Truth*:

"Homelessness is a weariness of spirit. It is the constant friction and tension of being misquoted or misunderstood. It is the restlessness that sets in from being a sojourner on this earth."[19] To clarify, the term *homeless* is not in any way meant to minimize the experience of people who suffer the agony of being physically unhoused. It names this lack of "social belonging," and how being misunderstood is the experience of the racial and ethnic minority. There is a similar feeling for those in the foster care system, those who are in abusive homes, or those in elderly care facilities—they are among the "homeless," too, in a psychological sense.

To define it another way, we're lacking "households," but not in the way we've traditionally thought of them, according to writer Andy Crouch. He calls a household "a community of recognition," where we feel seen and recognized. It is not the same as a family, though they are related. The single proximate cause of loneliness, according to Crouch, is a lack of such households.[20] In the United States, our social architecture, the way we live in communities and cities, is developed with entities separate from one another: shopping centers, schools, churches, entertainment areas. Each of these are in isolated buildings, spread out. This is also the way we live: separated, segmented, apart, alone, in our own bubbles not only physically but also in terms of living in unremitting tension. Modern nuclear households (two parents and their children in a household, as opposed to extended family) as we know them today weren't normative until after the Industrial Revolution. Biblical texts actually speak of households more than the nuclear family, with households being about clans and tribes, as in many cultures around the world.

For example, gathering all elderly people in nursing homes or group facilities might make economic sense but it does not actually socially integrate the elderly. In fact, it is not so much aging that contributes to loneliness in the older population as the lack of options, lack of work, and lack of agency and opportunity for decision-making.[21] This is because we look on aging as a liability as opposed to an asset—and even the use of these financial terms is reductive and dehumanizing.

Interestingly, according to Pew Research, the share of Americans who live in multigenerational households has more than doubled in the past fifty years, which amounts to nearly sixty million US residents as of March 2021. Much of this change is due to overall population growth, with growing numbers of foreign-born Asian, Black, and Hispanic Americans, who are more likely to live in multigenerational households. Twenty-six percent of Black Americans, 26 percent of Hispanic Americans, and 24 percent of Asians live in multigenerational households, compared to 13 percent of the white population, though this is growing among non-Hispanic white Americans also. This trend of living in multigenerational households has not peaked yet. The reasons provided for why most live in multigenerational households are financial, as well as caring for other family members.[22] And living in these kinds of households could help alleviate loneliness, as they are a potential source of support and that "community of recognition."

Throughout our world history, colonialism and forced displacement have led to a separation of cultural and ethnic groups, resulting in alienation and a loss of identity and home, as people were uprooted from their ancestral homelands. The transatlantic slave trade forced the migration of African populations, resulting in the creation of diaspora communities where individuals faced isolation and discrimination, and struggled to maintain connection to their cultures of origin. During World War II, Japanese Americans were forced into incarceration camps and experienced loss of homes and livelihoods. In various countries, including the United

States and Canada, Indigenous children were forcibly removed from their families and placed in boarding schools, resulting in erasure of their cultural identity. Holocaust survivors live with the trauma of genocide and displacement, and experienced cultural loneliness as they grappled with their identity and loss of home and family. The Chinese Exclusion Act of 1882 in the United States, the first major law restricting immigration based on ethnicity, resulted in feelings of exclusion and loneliness as Chinese immigrants faced discrimination. These examples illustrate systemic discrimination, forced isolation, cultural displacement, and the contribution to feelings of ethnic loneliness.

"Whatever belonging is, it involves belonging *with* and *to* others in a place," writes David P. Leong in *Race and Place*.[23] Land tells stories—stories of power and wealth, stories of belonging, exclusion, politics, economics. Humanity has lived in community through much of history because it was a necessity,[24] but now our communities have changed because of industrialization, westernization, white flight, redlining, gentrification, and more, to create segregation in our cities. But when we primarily experience belonging only in homogeneity (racial, cultural, religious, or otherwise), we are missing out on transformative community. "The story of race is also the story of place," writes Dr. Willie Jennings.[25] We don't live in proximity in our cities, which are largely segregated; in fact, our "most diverse cities are often the most segregated."[26] Our stories of belonging are deeply entrenched in place—and we are lonely in those places.

## STRANGERS ON EARTH

When God told Abraham to leave Ur (Mesopotamia) for a new land (Canaan), he was telling Abraham to leave his homeland and all that was familiar. Abraham was over seventy years old and was told to leave his father's house and relatives (Gen 12:1). He didn't know where he was going (Heb 11:8); he had no map, no relatives in the area, no GPS, no rest stops or tea stalls, and no hotels. He did have an entourage of one thousand people walking on foot, as well as animals. When Abraham left his homeland, becoming an immigrant, God told the Hebrews how they were to treat the foreigners and strangers: "The foreigner residing among you must be treated as your native-born. Love them as yourself, for you were foreigners in Egypt" (Lev 19:34).

The story of the Israelites' exodus from Egypt highlights the experience of displacement and disbelonging during their forty years of wandering in the wilderness, and a yearning for a homeland and belonging. During their years of wandering, God provided provision in the form of manna, and protection by his presence in the form of a pillar of cloud by day and a pillar of fire by night. During those years, God provided them a set of laws to help them live in community with one another and with God. God promised to deliver them to a land they could call home.

In these stories of displacement, God promises to deliver and protect. Likewise, in our own stories of displacement, migration, and diaspora, amid our earthly wanderings and dwellings, God longs to lead us to a place of rest and home—an eternal rest, and a place of spiritual rest for our weary souls. Perhaps our journeys of ethnic loneliness are also wilderness wanderings where God is standing near to deliver us with promises of rest and home. Perhaps God is standing nearby—and we've focused on the wilderness instead of the pillar of fire and cloud. Today, we move and resettle all over the earth, some of us voluntarily and millions of others of us forcibly displaced. No matter where we live, we share a common identity as foreigners and exiles on earth (1 Pet 2:11), and as sojourners with eyes set on a heavenly place (Phil 3:20).

Jesus also didn't have his own home; he was literally homeless. When someone once approached him, saying he'd follow him anywhere, Jesus responded by telling him this is the cost: there will be no home, no place of comfort, and many unknowns. Basically, he's asking the man, *Are you sure you want to join me and be homeless too?* He said of himself, "Foxes have dens and birds have nests, but the Son of Man has no place to lay his head" (Luke 9:58). Jesus knew what it was like to be homeless, as a function of his ambulatory ministry. Yet, though Jesus was homeless as an itinerant preacher, he also knew the hospitality of those who welcomed and hosted him and experienced the generosity of those who opened their homes. He experienced the homelessness and loneliness of being on earth while waiting to abide in eternity with God. He understands our waiting, our restlessness, our longings for home, and our quest to belong.

• • •

In June 1969, when my parents set foot in the United States for the first time, some kind folks offered them help: someone gave them furniture, and a colleague took my parents on their first grocery shopping trip in the United States. The colleague also lent my father two hundred dollars so he could buy a car (it was an old beat-up Dodge with torn seats and exposed springs, which he purchased for $75). My father also bought a black-and-white TV for one hundred dollars because they wanted to see the first astronauts landing on the moon. My parents lived in a small apartment in New Jersey, and my mom (though she had been exposed to some English writing and reading in school) learned how to speak fluent English by watching *I Love Lucy* on that black-and-white TV. Lucy's comedic antics transcended language.

It takes courage to step into the newness of leaving the comforts of all that is familiar, to move from one home to another, saying *I belong here.* It takes courage to define what your new "home" may look like to you, in the context of your ethnic and racial identity.

So, what am I? I am a pilgrim who's known a feeling of rootlessness and who longs for a sense of belonging. I am Alabama clay mixed with the dust of India, sandalwood, and honeysuckle, and my tears are mixed with sugar cane and monsoon rains. I am on a quest for home.

## SO, WHAT ARE YOU?

You have a place
You are tethered by geography
You are not the first
To be misunderstood
To feel rootless, roofless
Homeless
You are not the first
Nor will you be the last
To experience loneliness
You are not alone
In the Land of Loneliness
You will find
Home again
You will be at home
Wherever you find yourself

## QUESTIONS FOR REFLECTION AND DISCUSSION

1. What does home mean to you? Define home and the concept of home. Do you feel at home where you are? Why or why not?

2. Writing prompts:
   - "After I began searching for home . . ."
   - "I think home should be . . ."

3. Describe your family. Do you or your family live in a multi-generational household?

4. Draw your family tree. Use creative license: use drawings, symbols, pictures. It doesn't have to look like a traditional tree. What do you notice about your tree? What gaps and holes exist? What new things are you learning about your background?

5. Read the poem "Where I'm From" by George Ella Lyon here: www.georgeellalyon.com/where.html. After you read the poem, try writing your own (the website link has ideas for how to do this).[27]

# 3

# BEAUTY, BELONGING, AND IDENTITY THEFT

*He who is different from me*
*does not impoverish me—he enriches me.*

ANTOINE DE SAINT-EXUPÉRY

My small southern school organized beauty pageants. From seventh grade onward, students listed the names of girls they thought were the prettiest in their grade on a secret ballot. Yes, it was an annual voted-in-by-peers beauty contest. The girls with the most votes would be in the upcoming pageant. The results were tallied and posted in the hallway. I'd nonchalantly saunter over to the posting each year and review the names on the list, even though I already knew the answer.

The process of preparing for the pageant itself remained a mystery to me. How many evening gowns did one try on before choosing sparkly royal blue or a flouncy light pink? Did I miss a secret class for thirteen-year-olds on how to properly apply blush and eyeliner? I only possessed a rudimentary pile of eyeshadow and lip gloss. How does one become beautiful—and discover the secret formula to be voted in? I knew girls would "lay out" in the sun to get a tan, because they didn't want pale skin, but they were choosing when they wanted to be Brown. Otherwise, who chooses Brown? I couldn't choose.

In elementary school, where my sister and I were the only Asian Indian students, each morning my mother divided my long hair into two sections, braiding my hair into two braids, weaving a red ribbon through the braids, and then tying the braids into two loops, one on each side of my head, just as girls would wear in India.

The problem was we weren't in India.

No one else wore their hair like mine in my southern school. When I was in sixth grade, I wanted to wear my hair down, because I was too old for ribbons and braids and I wanted to look like everyone else. My hair, however, was not straight like most other Indian girls—mine was naturally curly and, hence, very tangly. I didn't know how to tame my hair or that something called "conditioner" existed. In India, women used coconut oil in their hair, but nobody I knew used that in America. Other kids already called me names such as "mophead," making fun of me and my hair. I didn't want to add coconut oil fuel to the fire.

Hair is a whole thing! I can't count how many times I visited a beauty salon and the hairdresser (who sees a lot of hair) would remark in wonder or dismay at how thick my hair was.

I imagined my life with blond hair, even seriously considering changing my hair color when I was older as a sort of unscientific experiment to compare my life before and after blond hair. If only I had the magic keys of blond hair and white skin, I thought my life would be easier.

I never made the "list," so I'd watch the beauty pageants as a spectator in the crowd, cheering for a friend or two. But it would be years before I cast a vote of belonging for myself.

As ethnic minorities, our sense of cultural identity is at risk because of cultural standards of beauty in white-majority spaces, threatening our sense of belonging. We live as perpetual foreigners, both invisible and hypervisible, while we navigate a process of identity negotiation with ourselves, our communities, and our culture at-large, contributing to our sense of ethnic loneliness.

## COLORISM

What the West defines as our standards of what is beautiful or handsome is a concept that has spread all across the globe, with a preference for lighter skin tones, a phenomenon called *colorism*. The concept of colorism exists worldwide, resulting in "a global, mass-marketed phenomenon that has been spread through colonization and continues to be spread via the television, film, music, and advertising industries." Brands like Vaseline and L'Oréal offer products and advertisements promoting the idea that light skin color is the solution to our problems of belonging.[1] So whether I'd grown up in India or the United States, I wouldn't have escaped this mentality.

Notably, though, the world's largest market for skin-lightening products is in India, where "there is a strong preference for light skin or 'fairness.'" This preference did not occur "until the 15th and 16th centuries—when contact with Europe increased."[2] In India, many marriages are still arranged, and as matchmakers and family members seek matrimonial matches for their children, the biodata of eligible folks includes age, height, education, and—you guessed it—skin tone. By and large, fair-skinned women are preferred, and skin color is a deliberate point of discussion.

But India isn't alone. Skin-lightening creams are among the top-selling cosmetic products in Africa, Latin America, and other parts of Asia. Approximately one-third to one-half of women in Africa are estimated to use skin-lightening creams; in Nigeria it is estimated to be up to 77 percent. The idea of light skin as synonymous with ideals of beauty has resulted in billion-dollar industries and a "form of social capital for women." These privileges "come at the cost of isolation, invisibility, and loss of identity."[3]

The issues of appearance don't only apply to women but also to men, just in a different way. Asian men, for example, are depicted as weak and less favored as the male romantic lead in media. For example, a musical from a popular Bollywood movie is scheduled to be the first Bollywood musical on Broadway, and the female lead is an Indian actor, but the male lead they chose is white.[4]

There are also general classist assumptions underneath colorism, with the idea that darker skin is associated with working-class field laborers, who work outdoors in the sun. Fair skin is associated with being indoors and belonging to a higher class/caste. Whenever I visit India, comments about the fairness or darkness of someone's skin occur in some context or another.

## THE PERPETUAL FOREIGNER

My parents and I, along with my brother and his family, visited North India in April 2022. It had been the first visit to North India in seventeen years for my parents and twenty-seven years for me, which is a very long time to go without seeing one's extended family. I saw aunts, uncles, cousins, and my cousins' children whom I had never met. In addition to visiting as many relatives as possible and attending a wedding, my mother had a special request: to see the Taj Mahal, a place she had never seen before. So, we made a day trip from Delhi to Agra during our stay. A record-breaking heat wave held firm, with temperatures no less than 103 degrees and up to 111 degrees Fahrenheit, yet we were determined to go. When we got our tickets for the Taj Mahal, the ticket dealers asked if we were from India. Yes, my parents answered, and then we were asked to show passports. But because we are all US citizens and possess US passports, we didn't qualify as "Indian" and had to pay tourist fees and prices. It didn't matter that my parents were born in India. This was quite the turnaround for them—to be labeled "tourists"in the land of their birth and childhood. My mom remarked, "We are tourists when we visit India, and we are immigrants in America."The disbelonging goes both ways—a visitor here, and a visitor there. *Perpetual foreigners.*

*Perpetual*: consistent, usual, eternal, forever, incessant, changeless, persistent, always, unchanging. Perpetual, like the seasons, like the sun rising and setting, the phases of the moon, the clouds, the weather, like taxes, like waves crashing on a shore.

*Foreigner*: alien, stranger, other, immigrant, refugee, international, undocumented, illegal, unknown, outsider, nonresident, nonnative, foreign-born. The opposite of a comfort zone, of being known, the opposite of rest and relief, the opposite of safety. Elicits questions, curiosity, fear, doubt, anger, exclusion.

Mix and match the nouns and adjectives. A constant stranger. An eternal immigrant. The forever other. Consistently outside. Persistently unknown. Always an alien. Notice the words related to *perpetual* include absolutes, such as *always* or *forever*. In healthy, mutual conversation, we are advised not to use terms such as *you always* or *you never* because they degenerate conversation instead of moving the dialogue forward to greater understanding. These terms assume that there is an either/or scenario and leave no room for common ground or nuance. You either belong, or you don't. You're either a foreigner, or you aren't. The term *foreigner* implies "otherness."

The term *perpetual foreigner* refers to a situation where ethnic and cultural minority groups are regularly perceived as outsiders, no matter how many generations we can trace back our presence or our citizenship. A psychological study conducted in 2011 gathered responses from Asian American, Latin American, and African American participants, and concluded that the perpetual foreigner stereotype was connected to identity conflict, a lower sense of belonging to American culture, lower life satisfaction for Asian Americans, and higher rates of depression for Latin Americans. In addition, research found that even perceived discrimination is a predictor of depression and anxiety for African American adults, and is related to lowered hope.[5] Being seen as primarily "foreign" in every personal or professional capacity takes a terrible toll.

Folks who identify as mixed race or multiethnic don't really know where to fit in—which race should they choose, or which culture? They experience a "perpetual sense of displacement," as explained by Chandra Crane in *Mixed Blessing*.[6] Many say they aren't fully at home in their own skin, feeling a *constant* sense of "otherness." It wasn't until 1960 that folks could choose their own race on the census, and 2000 that Americans could choose more than one race. According to Pew Research, "In the mid-19th century, for example, some race scientists theorized that multiracial children of black and white parents were genetically inferior, and sought statistical evidence in the form of census data to back up their theories." Racism was built into the census forms. In fact, it is possible to view the changes in terminology on the census forms from 1790 to today.[7]

To be a perpetual foreigner is to consistently feel a sense of disbelonging or alienation from community or society, living on the edges, fences, or perimeters, unsure of when to step a foot from one side to the other. Not fully being seen, known, or belonging in one's culture and not being fully accepted in the culture at-large, perpetual foreigners are othered, contributing to loneliness.

## "IDENTITY THEFT" AND GHOST LIVES

When my parents immigrated to the United States from India, they gradually put aside many of their traditional practices and customs. Living as immigrants in small towns and rural areas, away from other Asian Indians in particular, left my family in a position to assimilate in a different way than if we had settled in places with a higher Indian immigrant population, such as New Jersey, Chicago, or San Francisco. They didn't have a Hindu temple to visit or gather often with other Indian families (at least not until a few more families moved into the area as the years progressed). Indeed, with no other Indian community around, it was difficult to keep up with following traditions and customs. The busyness of surviving, living, and working was enough all by itself.

As people of color, immigrants, or children of immigrants, we set aside parts of ourselves and go about the tasks of daily living, surviving, assimilating. We stash away our culture, traditions, and identity. We dress in Western clothes, tucking any foreignness away like an undershirt, hiding anything "different" from the white-majority preference. Because we can't change our appearances, we change ourselves, covering up and hiding away those parts that are deemed "too foreign" or "too Brown" or "too Black." It is hard to be our complete, whole selves when the society we're in doesn't see us as complex individuals made in God's image. Perhaps there is also a failure here to appreciate the complexity of God?

When we can't fully be ourselves, it's a stunted existence. We can't fully belong, because we're afraid of what ire our full identities will provoke and of alienating ourselves further. We experience the pain of saying goodbye to ourselves as we knew ourselves—the other selves. How does one hide, or say goodbye, without some measure of pain? People who have lost limbs sometimes complain of "ghost pains"—they feel the pain of that limb as if it were still attached. Saying goodbye to a part of ourselves is like feeling that "ghost pain" of another self that once existed. This is a kind of "identity theft," different from the kind when someone steals our social security number and personal data and impersonates us. This kind of identity theft signifies a loss of identity—an erasure—in which parts of our story are forgotten, hidden, and stuffed away, and we attempt to construct a form out of this unexplainable existence.[8] Our narratives are defined by this bifurcation. Thus, there are millions of ghost lives missing from the lives of ethnic and racial minorities, as we've cut off parts of our identities to assimilate, attempt to belong, or were forcibly removed from our lands, displaced, relocated, or enslaved.

The less we understand about a disease or symptom, the more we stigmatize it. Meghan O'Rourke writes, "If medicine can't see or name the problem, it can neither study it nor treat it."[9] Likewise, if society is unwilling to recognize or name the pathology of ethnic loneliness, and the systems that persist behind it, we will struggle to treat it.

Racism, like an undefined chronic illness, does not have a definite cure date. Some folks will say they aren't racist, or they've had a training or conversation about it, and it's done. This is akin to treating a symptom and not the disease itself. The fact is, one conversation, a Diversity, Equity, and Inclusion training, or not overtly "doing anything bad" doesn't mean we don't have some kind of bias or are not contributing to the problem or being complicit in some way.

We are all one in the body of Christ: "Just as a body, though one, has many parts, but all its many parts form one body, so it is with Christ. For we were all baptized by one Spirit so as to form one body—whether Jews or Gentiles, slave or free—and we were all given the one Spirit to drink. Even so the body is not made up of one part but of many" (1 Cor 12:12-14). And if one part of us hurts, we all hurt. "If one part suffers, every part suffers with it; if one part is honored, every part rejoices with it" (1 Cor 12:26). The ghost pains of identities stolen and lost reverberate through our land and affect us all.

## CONNECTING WITH OUR
## CULTURAL IDENTITIES

Our sense of self in connection to our cultural or ethnic group and our cultural identity plays a significant role in shaping our experiences. Our cultural identity offers us a sense of belonging in society, as well as a support system and an emotional connection with those who have similar cultural experiences. A strong sense of cultural identity can also empower us to resist pressure to assimilate all of ourselves and to share and promote our cultural heritage. As minorities, we navigate a process of identity negotiation, balancing our own cultural identity with those of the dominant culture. This negotiation impacts our sense of belonging and how we are perceived by others.

When we consider our intersecting identities (gender, ethnicity, cultural heritage), it amplifies our loneliness, especially for those of us who belong to multiple marginalized groups (such as being both female and Black). This magnifies the sense of loneliness we feel, because we are dealing with marginalization and discrimination from multiple angles, compounding our sense of isolation. Furthermore, a lack of representation or role models with these intersecting identities leads to a feeling of invisibility. With multiple intersecting marginalized identities, there is a greater risk of misunderstandings and misinterpretations— and loneliness.

I remember hearing in church that in the ancient world of the New Testament, a Jewish man would give thanks that he was not born a woman. I wondered if Asian Indian men might think the same way, since Indian society is rife with patriarchy. Despite the fact India had a female prime minister decades ago, and women in middle and upper classes are encouraged to pursue an education, men typically enjoy a higher status in society, and women deal on a wide scale with issues such as discrimination, bias, domestic abuse, dowry deaths, sexual abuse, and female infanticide. A man born in India, then, could repeat what the Jewish man said: "Thank God I wasn't born a woman." What would American men say?

Moreover, individuals with multiple minority identities have limited support networks, and experience greater social isolation. Navigating spaces that are predominantly representative of only one of their identities creates a greater sense of isolation and othering. The cumulative effect of all of these stressors can have a significant impact on mental health. It is ironic to consider that we feel both hypervisible and invisible, as we are treated both as a stranger and as someone who is easily targeted. Our minority status puts us in a peculiar, liminal, in-between space.

## INVISIBILITY AND HYPERVISIBILITY

"Nobody called to check on me," Mindy shared through tears during a Zoom conversation one afternoon. Mindy, who is from the Philippines, had raised her family in Arizona among a small tight-knit group of white friends. For thirty years, they raised their children and celebrated life together with backyard barbecues, playdates, and church. A few weeks after the Atlanta shooting occurred in March 2021, in which six women of Asian descent were massacred, Mindy confessed that some of her closest friends in that group had not reached out to her or thought to ask how she was doing after that attack. On social media, folks were encouraging each other to "check on their Asian friends," and Mindy harbored hope and expectation she'd hear from some of her closest friends. Why had they not thought to reach out to her? How had they not known she was hurting—or thought to check if she was? Their lack of recognizing the pain she felt at the horrific shooting left Mindy feeling lonely and isolated from the group. Mindy admitted she sometimes felt like the "token Asian" in their group, and other times she felt as if her friends didn't notice or acknowledge her Asian identity.

I attended a class not too long ago with about ten other students on the Japanese art of taking care of bonsai trees. I don't recall the instructor ever saying my name aloud, but he knew my name and knew who I was only because I stood out as the only woman of color in the group. In our last class the instructor was handing out certificates, and he didn't know who was who among the white male attendees in the class—but he knew who I was. The only reason he knew my name, I am aware, was because I have a unique name and I looked different from everyone else. When it was obvious that the instructor knew who I was and passed my certificate to me, one of the white guys called me a "teacher's pet." It took me by surprise. There was absolutely no reason for me to be called a "teacher's pet." We had all been in the class together at the same time, meeting once a month for six months. Immediately I felt the eyes of the rest of the classmates on me, as if this comment suggested some sort of special treatment. Not only was he incorrect, but I wanted to clarify to the classmate the only reason my name was known (but not even spoken aloud) is because I was the woman of color with a foreign name, and it was obvious. It didn't mean I was the "teacher's pet"—it just meant I couldn't hide. This wasn't an isolated incident. It's repeated when I am the only woman of color at a gathering. My presence is noted, it is immediate and known, and sometimes it is mistaken or misconstrued. You can't hide even when you want to hide, and sometimes false assumptions are made.

There is tension between invisibility and hypervisibility. Often both realities are present at once. On the one hand, people of color can be invisible and overlooked and ignored in ways that diminish our influence and humanity. On the other hand, we are conspicuously visible and can't hide from our ethnicity in white-majority spaces, and thus get targeted and profiled.

While we experience varying levels of invisibility, ironically, we also experience stereotyping, discrimination, prejudice, and exclusion—which means we are noticed but not seen in the way we want to be seen. Furthermore, even the *possibility* of stereotyping and discrimination can affect our psychological and physical well-being.[10]

## A LANGUAGE OF BELONGING

In Indian culture, we grow up calling all our elders *uncle* and *auntie*, even those we are not biologically related to. *Everyone* is an uncle or an aunt. Adults refer to all younger folk as children, or *betah*. We refer to our siblings, cousins, and all of our peers as *brother* and *sister*. The Indian subcontinent thus consists of many brothers and sisters, uncles and aunties. Because the way we think of one another is built into the language, in essence, the entire Indian subcontinent is one extended family.

In her book *See No Stranger*, activist and attorney Valarie Kaur challenges us to see each other with a sense of wonder, with these words: "You are a part of me I do not yet know." The South African word *Ubuntu* means "I am because you are." In Sanskrit, the words *Tat Tvam asi* mean "I am that," a term used to refer to one another.[11]

These words mean we belong to each other. Loneliness arises when those around us look at us and say the opposite. This is true for anyone who feels marginalized: not just those of another skin color but also other marginalized groups, such as those who are disabled, neurodivergent, or LGBTQ+. What in our modern language today can serve to foster a sense of belonging? Is it love? How can we reimagine our language to conceptualize the idea that we truly belong to one another, that we are all parts of one another that we do not yet know?

## AS-IS

In the survey I conducted, one respondent said they feel alienated when "people assume I wouldn't try something new because of their preconceived idea of what a Black person does or doesn't do." It's one thing to be known and rejected, and another thing entirely to be rejected or misunderstood without being known at all. When a room full of strangers immediately sizes me up based on my skin color or appearance, I experience a more profound loneliness.

To fully acknowledge our longing to belong and to be known, at some point we must have understood we did not belong. People can spend a lifetime not being known, surrounded by other people, living with others, working with others, in regular contact with others, but still unknown.

The ethnic minority living in a white-majority space walks through life on a regular basis with that feeling of being unknown by the culture and society at-large. Being unknown means that our existence, stories, songs, culture, language, and values have been flattened or erased to stereotypes, caricatures, news events, headlines, and one-dimensional narratives.

This sort of rejection does not allow for the opportunity to discover deep soul friendship, the "anam cara," or "soul friend" as John O'Donohue describes, calling this type of soul friendship "an act of recognition and belonging."[12] Another survey respondent who identified as of Black/African descent commented, "When you're the only one (or one of a few), it's easy for you to get singled out and/or have to be the face for your people. This was and is difficult especially if people have opinions of your race based on their biases."

What might a soul friendship look like with people who look different from us? As an ethnic minority, I know how often we ask this question both in imagination and in practice, as we are nearly always the minority in a majority space in the US context. One way might be for dominant culture folks to ask themselves how their privilege might be a barrier to someone else in this space, or to ask how they can befriend someone without minimizing their minority experience. We are all seeking to transcend the bounds of isolation.

Being known means not having to pretend. It means living with a strong enough sense of safety that we feel free to be who we are, as we are, without risking rejection or ostracization because of our differences in skin color, ethnicity, or culture. It means we are allowed to be ourselves. But I do want to add a caveat to the minority reader: be safe. There are levels to safety and belonging—and your ability to be "as-is" will vary with your circumstances and environment. You can be true to a version of yourself—and it doesn't mean you are inauthentic. It means you recognize the reality that your ability to be authentic is "informed by self-preservation and sense of safety."[13]

## PERPETUALLY KNOWN

A strong relationship exists between a person's sense of belonging and her sense of happiness and well-being. A study of college students found that depression, loneliness, and anxiety greatly reduced how often the students experienced a sense of belonging.[14] Consider that fact now in light of the statistic that more than one in three international students feel friendless and long for more meaningful relationships with Americans. I have also heard (though the number is hard to quantify and verify) the majority of international students never see the inside of an American home.[15]

When ethnic minorities are not part of community and are unable to partake in the give-and-take of living in relationship, both sides suffer and community cannot flourish. Jesus exhorts us to love our neighbor as we love ourselves. We are part of one another, but many Christians have been taught a Western, individualized gospel that extols an individualized experience of salvation and transformation at the neglect of the communal aspects of faith.[16] Yet we find that the Old Testament mentions immigrants (*ger* in Hebrew) ninety-two times.[17] Beginning in 800 BC, the Jewish prophets emphasized that the quality of faith in the people depended on the character of the justice of the land, and that character is judged by how we take care of the most vulnerable in society: the widows, orphans, and strangers.[18] "This is not a liberal agenda item," writes Ronald Rolheiser in *The Holy Longing*. "It is something that lies at the very heart of the gospel and which Jesus himself makes the ultimate criterion for our final judgment."[19] God cares about justice. It isn't a passing or minor issue: it's a major one.

"The wisdom across faith traditions is that grieving is done in community," writes Valarie Kaur.[20] In fact, in the Bible, the commands in Scripture are written most often in the second person plural: "you all." This suggests a collective teaching and response—not an individualistic one as our modern society's interpretations would have us believe.[21] Yet in the United States, we grieve privately and do not have a ritual for grief or loss when someone passes away, but lamenting together over our losses and trials is one way we draw together in community.

We are bumping elbows and sharing space with other folks navigating this wilderness. While we ethnic minorities may be perpetually "unknown" on earth, we are "perpetually" seen, known, and loved by God. God knows us, our beginnings, our futures, our names, our hearts, our concerns, our thoughts, our actions, our weaknesses and loves us as-is. J. I. Packer, in *Knowing God*, explains it this way:

> What matters supremely, therefore, is not, in the last analysis, the fact that I know God, but the larger fact which underlies it—the fact that *he knows me*.... There is no moment when

his eye is off me, or his attention distracted from me, and no moment, therefore, when his care falters. . . . His love to me is utterly realistic, based at every point on prior knowledge of the worst about me, so that no discovery now can disillusion him about me, in the way I am so often disillusioned about myself, and quench his determination to bless me.[22]

So, what could our standards of belonging be instead of external appearance? Perhaps our standards are that we belong to each other, that "I am because you are," *Tat Tvam asi*, that each person is not only our neighbor but our family—that being human is enough to belong.

Our task and message to each other in the BIPOC community is to remind each other that this place of marginalization isn't a desolate, barren place. It's the soil where dreams are made and cultivated. Our cultural identities are places of beauty and reclamation—places where we learn to reclaim ourselves and the truth of who we are.

• • •

Moses was born to Hebrew parents but was raised as an Egyptian prince in Pharaoh's palace. As he grew older, he became aware of his Hebrew heritage and faced an identity crisis—an internal conflict between his Egyptian upbringing and his Hebrew roots. Perhaps he felt a sense of identity confusion and felt disconnected from both sides of his heritage. After he killed an Egyptian taskmaster, Moses spent years in exile, away from his previous life in Egypt and contending with his identity. When God called him to lead the Israelites out of Egypt, he returned to Egypt to confront Pharaoh, and had to contend with his dual identity and his mission to liberate the Hebrew people. But this unique bicultural identity is what made him the right leader. His gifts were found in this dual identity: Moses was a Hebrew, and he understood the inner workings of Pharaoh's court. Likewise, for us, we have gifts to offer from our diverse perspectives. Our abilities to navigate different worlds are unique gifts and contributions we have to offer the world.

God wants to redeem your ethnicity and show you your place of belonging in this world. As we move toward wholeness, it means seeking those places where we've let go of pieces of our cultural belonging and identity. To live wholly and fully means naming and addressing those parts of our identity we have left behind in order to assimilate or belong. How can we integrate and live authentically, without giving up who we are? Living authentically and in peace with ourselves, others, and God is crucial to our healing, because no matter when the dominant culture chooses to accept or not accept us, we must live in peace with ourselves.

## SO, WHAT ARE YOU?

The standard of belonging
Is not based on your outward appearance
Your skin color, stature, or eye shape
You are targeted
By God's lovingkindness
You are not a monolith
You are not a myth
You are magnificent
In the margins
Our differences are delights
And enriching
You who long to belong
Have a place among

The family of humanity
In the darkness of disbelonging
There exists the beauty of belonging

## QUESTIONS FOR REFLECTION
## AND DISCUSSION

1. What standards of beauty have you internalized from the
   majority culture? Have you wanted to reject your background,
   race, culture, accent, or some other part of your identity? In a
   journal or small group, explain that feeling. Do you still feel
   that way? Explain.

2. Writing prompts:
   - "Something beautiful about me is . . ."
   - "I want to be perpetually known for . . ."

3. In what ways have you been a perpetual foreigner to yourself
   and the ways God has designed you?

4. Do you feel any part of your identity was stolen or lost?
   Explain.

# 4

# ISOLATED AND OTHERED

*Alone, all alone*
*Nobody, but nobody*
*Can make it out here alone.*

MAYA ANGELOU

Pick a color," she said. "Write down your color." I was at a writers' workshop in Minnesota, and this was our prompt. I wrote down "pink." *No one else will pick that color*, I thought to myself. Then we were told our assignment: head outdoors and look for the color we had chosen.

I couldn't find anything pink. It was cloudy, with no streaks of a pinkish sunset brushing the sky. I spotted peach-colored rasp-berries ripening on the vine. Spiky lavender thistle blooms swayed high above the grasses. I detected tiny maroon slivers of crushed stones in the concrete road. Otherwise, I was surrounded by swaths of green grass and leafing trees in shades of emerald, jade, lime, pistachio, sage, and artichoke. No pink anywhere.

*Should I change my color? No one would know.*

*No, I'll be honest and stick with pink.*

Then I remembered a science lesson. The color we see with the naked eye is the hue that is *not* absorbed by the object; what we see is the color reflected back to us. Green leaves and grasses absorb every color in the spectrum except green, so what I see bouncing back to my eyes is green. That meant pink really was everywhere, even if my human eyes could not see it.

Similarly, when I see your face, I see dimly. I can't see your past, but if I'm paying attention, I might detect bits of joy flashing when your eyes light up. I can't see your thoughts—though sometimes your emotions give themselves away. Sometimes, we only reflect back to others what we want them to see. Sometimes we think what we can see with our human eyes is all there is. Sometimes all others see is "different," when there are really rich tones of melanin and shades of brown reflecting back, with all of their accompanying tones, tints, stories, and songs.

## SEEING BEYOND STEREOTYPES

When I first moved to the Midwest from the South, people sometimes laughed or chuckled when I started talking because I had a slight, but recognizable, southern accent. Someone once flat-out started laughing uncontrollably. Years later I realized my missed opportunity: if all I had to do to make people laugh was open my mouth and start talking, I could have had a stellar career as a comedian. If you were trying to fit me into the Asian Indian stereotype, I was the anomaly, the outlier, the weird data point, with my southern accent and upbringing.

But that's just the thing. We should beware of this—the one narrative that transforms a group into a stereotype. "There is the danger of a single story," says novelist Chimimanda Ngozi Adichie, who spent her childhood in Nigeria. As a child, she wrote the same kinds of stories she read about: characters who ate apples and remarked about the snow, which is not at all how she lived in Nigeria. Once she discovered African writers, it saved her from having a single story about what stories could be and what books are.[1] Each ethnic group is made of multiple stories; we are more than a single narrative.

Sarah Shin, author of *Beyond Colorblind*, writes, "We need to become ethnicity aware in order to address the beauty and brokenness in our ethnic stories and the stories of others."[2] This kind of posture, which focuses on awareness and wonder, translates into asking questions, being curious, and not assuming a stereotype we've heard or seen is the identity of all people of color in a particular ethnic or racial group. Knowing us, the "minority," the "foreigner," means going beyond stereotypes and generalities. It leads us toward cultural appreciation, "valuing, affirming, and striving to support a culture *with all its nuance and complications*," writes Chandra Crane, multiethnic resource specialist and author of *Mixed Blessing*.[3]

## COLORBLINDNESS

Renee is a biracial Punjabi American with Irish, Polish, and French ancestry. She leads a consultancy that equips leaders in demonstrating culturally intelligent practices to deliver the outcomes of diversity, equity, inclusion, and belonging. When she was a baby, Renee was afraid of going to her uncles who were wearing turbans. When they removed their turbans, she was fine. She doesn't recall if she reacted similarly to uncles on the other side of her family who wore cowboy hats. Even as youngsters, we are not without biases.

In an attempt to not sound racist and to separate themselves from obviously racist individuals, some folks will say, "I'm colorblind." But the truth is we are not colorblind. Babies and children actually notice race at young ages—some studies indicate as early as three months. By nine months, babies use race to categorize faces, and by age three, children associate some races with negative traits.[4]

I've heard the idea that America is colorblind: *America elected a Black president, and therefore, we've overcome our obstacles.* Electing a

Black president is something many did not believe would occur in their lifetime, so does that now mean we've achieved racial equity? Electing a Black president did not change the fact that Black Americans are incarcerated at five times the rate of white Americans.[5] Electing a Black president did not radically alter the tragic number of police brutality cases against Black people. Likewise, just because we have neighbors in a racially mixed marriage, or a couple at our church adopted Black or Brown children, or we did so ourselves, does not mean that we've achieved ethnic and racial harmony. Proximity does not erase structural inequality.

We *can* see color, and the idea of colorblindness actually cloaks the real issues of living in a racialized society and the systems perpetuating it. Colorblindness doesn't work toward injustice. It may be well-intentioned, but colorblindness actually causes harm. "Colorblindness has a kind of homogenizing effect on communities: it suggests unity through uniformity instead of belonging in spite of difference," according to David P. Leong, author of *Race and Place*.[6] Instead, we are "color-blessed," as Dr. Derwin Gray, pastor, author, and former NFL player, says.[7]

## MODEL MINORITY MYTH

"Do you know Dr. [insert any Indian American doctor's name here]? You look just like her. She's a great doctor."

I've been asked this question more than a handful of times in my life. It's usually a stranger, such as a clerk in a store or a passerby. After I admit I'm not the individual in question, nor do I know the individual in question, the other party will usually explain what they appreciate about their doctor. Thankfully I've only been mistaken for "good" doctors thus far!

I grew up as a member of a group affected by the model minority myth, which is a category particular to the Asian American population. I didn't know I belonged to this group, nor did I know such a group had a name. No one had articulated this persona or stereotype directly to me, nor was it written down anywhere that I had read, but I knew it simply by observing and through experience. Only years later would I learn it had a name.

The model minority myth perpetuates a stereotype that Asians, in particular, excel in academics, math, science, and music. The myth describes Asians as exemplary, law-abiding, subservient, courteous citizens, who have achieved success through innate abilities or hard work, and are often held up as the "ideal immigrant" or "ideal Asian." One harm is that this stereotype erases the differences among individuals. Consider the heterogeneity of Asian Americans, who come from over twenty different countries. In the United States, Chinese Americans are the largest group, with Indian Americans next, followed by Filipino Americans, Vietnamese Americans, Korean Americans, and Japanese Americans, then another thirteen groups.[8] Saying all Asians have some kind of innate ability to be "successful" erases the experience of the vast majority of Asians. Are all white Americans "successful"? Are all white Americans the same? Of course not. The fact is that Asian Americans have the greatest income disparity of any other ethnic group in the United States. Asian Americans are both at the bottom and the top of the income distribution.[9]

Another harm is that the model minority myth makes false comparisons with other ethnic or racial groups. It has especially been weaponized against Black Americans "to argue that racism, including more than two centuries of black enslavement, can be overcome by hard work and strong family values."[10] This is a denial of the historical structural systems established in society that have prevented the African American and other populations access to the same privileges granted to the white population and other groups.

By 2055, Asian Americans are projected to be the largest immigrant group in the United States, surpassing Latin Americans.[11] Catherine Ceniza Choy, in her book *Asian American Histories of the United States*, writes that although there is great heterogeneity and diversity in the Asian American population, there are three areas that Asians have in common: violence, erasure, and resistance.[12] As Asians, in particular, our invisibility often results from being lumped into homogeneous groups or stereotypical groups, such as the model minority, and also through larger conversations about race consisting of a white-Black binary. This does not mean our Black brothers and sisters have it better; rather, that the dialogue historically has been about Black and white divides. Because Asians do not fit in either the Black or white race category, they are often left out of the conversation.

Asian Americans also have the highest poverty rate in New York City.[13] Most people are surprised by this statistic, because the model minority myth has been so deeply embedded in the media and accepted as "fact" in American society. Paradoxically, although Asians are seen as assimilating well, they still remain "hidden" and misunderstood, are considered "foreigners," erased, yet visibly targeted for hate crimes, as the upsurge of violent attacks on Asian Americans during the Covid-19 pandemic indicates.

While the model minority myth may be particular to Asian Americans, the core issue itself is not. All racial and ethnic groups—Latin Americans, African Americans, Indigenous peoples, etc.—are distinctive groups with unique attributes, and they deserve to have that individuality recognized rather than have generalizations imposed on them. Otherwise, the minority group is lumped together into a "monolith," contributing to the erasure of our unique identities and thus furthering marginalization, alienation, and loneliness.

## WAYS WE COPE

My friend Leslie ministers to and serves immigrants, refugees, and displaced persons in her community in the United States, developing friendships, meeting them for coffee, practicing English, and sometimes running errands or taking them to the doctor. In most cases, she is the only American friend they have. She is friends with a group of about a half dozen Syrian women who are always together. This group of Syrian women raise their kids together, talk together, share food and life. But beyond this group, they have few American friends, though they may know a few other Americans and other people. It's wonderful that they have each other and can support each other. But they also need friends beyond their own group.

A report called *The Belonging Barometer: The State of Belonging in America* found that a majority of Americans have a sense of disbelonging: 64 percent report not belonging in their workplace, 68 percent report not belonging in the nation, and 74 percent report not belonging in their community; 20 percent feel no sense of belonging in any of the life settings surveyed. Many report being treated "less-than," especially younger first-generation or noncitizen immigrants, Hispanic individuals, and gender minorities. And interestingly, the report found that belonging and diversity are interdependent. Americans with one or more diverse friends report higher levels of friendship belonging, and Americans in diverse neighborhoods report less marginalization if they experience local belonging.[14]

Upon arriving in the United States, my parents had only a few suitcases and no family or friends when they landed on the shores of New York. It's a tremendous sacrifice for those from other countries who come from societies with a strong sense of community, collectivist cultures, and large extended, close families. In fact, this is quite a salient point in the United States, which has the highest number of immigrants compared to any other country in the world: forty-five million people (as of 2019).[15] But this also applies to other regions and countries of the world that have opened their doors to thousands of refugees and displaced peoples.

I admire the resilience of our parents' generation and their re-solve to fit in. Yet, I also realize for that generation, the easiest path (and expectation) was not to create a fuss, to plow forward quietly, conduct their work diligently, and strive to provide a new life for their families and future generations: that path was as-similation. Assimilation asks us to leave our cultures and ethnic identities behind and embrace the culture of the land we inhabit. Assimilation involves rejecting our own cultures and embracing wholly the culture of the majority. As a consequence, we experience the grief of that loss.

We ethnic minorities, who are suffering the losses of what was left behind or what was stolen, who are alienated from society through systemic oppression, sometimes seek life in our own ethnic enclaves. Ethnic enclaves, which provide necessary community and a safe place to be one's full ethnic self, also magnify the isolation and loneliness from the rest of society.

Besides assimilation, as minorities, we employ various strategies to help us navigate (usually white-majority) spaces and new envi-ronments. With assimilation, we are balancing and trading off our heritage and identity. With integration, we are seeking to strike a balance between preserving our own cultural identity and living in majority culture; it's a two-way process involving effort from both the minority individual as well as the host society. As part of the minority group, we become accustomed to adopting a learning posture and a stance of cultural humility as we learn to adapt—but we all do this with varying degrees of acceptance. Often we have no choice but to do so. As we navigate spaces and learn to manage cultural changes and the dominant culture, we can experience any of the following:

- *Culture shock.* This results when adapting to new cultural norms, and creates feelings of disorientation, frustration, and loneliness.
- *Loss of familiarity.* Missing native and cultural foods, traditions, and environments contributes to homesickness and loneliness.
- *Value conflicts.* Differing cultural values can cause a clash with an individual or their community, society, church community, or within oneself, causing ethical dilemmas and internal conflicts.
- *Cultural misinterpretation.* We can misinterpret cultural cues or meanings and unintentionally offend or create confusion in social interactions and interpersonal communication.
- *Loss of cultural heritage.* Living with a fear of (or actual) loss of one's cultural identity creates distress and feelings of loneliness.
- *Employment challenges.* Learning workplace norms could affect the ability to advance in one's career.
- *Loss of social support.* Being separated from one's social network creates loneliness and emotional distress.
- *Isolation.* Differences can create feelings of being an outsider.
- *Parenting challenges.* Parents may face challenges in balancing cultural preservation and integration while raising their children, as well as teaching children how to address prejudice or bias they may encounter in school.
- *Balancing a dual identity.* This can lead to stress while adapting and interacting in multiple cultural frameworks.
- *Communication styles.* Differences in communication styles, such as directness or indirectness, can lead to misunderstandings and confusion.

- *Changing perceptions of home.* Shifting cultural contexts change our perception of what feels like "home," affecting our sense of belonging.

Just looking at the list makes me tired! Some of this is done subconsciously; some we are more aware of. Yet, these are some of the challenges ethnic and racial minority groups experience and navigate on a daily basis. And it can take a toll, affecting our physical and mental health.

## MENTAL HEALTH STIGMA

There are occasions when BIPOC want and need a mental health counselor who looks like them or is from the same cultural background. For the ethnic and racial minority, it can help to have a counselor or therapist belonging to the same racial or ethnic group, but finding therapists of color remains an obstacle—there aren't enough of them.

The stigma surrounding seeking mental health services and mental illness has improved in the United States in recent years, but that doesn't mean it's gone. The demand for mental health services increased substantially during and after the pandemic. In an article I wrote for *Sojourners* in 2021,[16] I shared a report that found one in five Asian Americans show signs of racial trauma.[17] But while 18 percent of the US population seeks mental health services, only 8.6 percent of Asian Americans do.[18] Barriers include the expectation to "just get over it," cultural expectations to rely on family instead of seeking help from a professional, stigma in the community for seeking mental health help, discrimination, and cultural assimilation, as well as the feeling that as a community, "we have encountered so much displacement, trauma, and discrimination [to assume] that it's just a normal part of life. We don't stop to deal with it—it's just the cost of living in the U.S. as an Asian

American," according to Liuan Huska, a Chicago-based writer.[19] But it's a critical issue because Asian American youth ages fifteen to twenty-four are the only racial group whose leading cause of death is suicide.[20]

A Black/African descent survey respondent shared the following story regarding her attendance at a conference on trauma in 2017:

> At lunch we were in line to get our food. I knew one person at the conference. A woman in front of me turned around and made conversation. She asked, "Were you sitting at the table near the large windows?" I answered, "No, I was sitting on the opposite side of the room with my friend." Then this woman responded, "Oh, I guess that's the other one." I knew she meant that's the other Black woman because there were two of us at the conference. I immediately felt shamed. I wanted to ask her "the other what?"

This respondent experienced the shame of being singled out—enduring her own trauma as a result. Mental health care for BIPOC individuals is a substantial need. In Appendix A, I share a list of BIPOC mental health resources as a starting point on finding mental health services.

## PARENTING IN A RACIALIZED SOCIETY

Recently a Twitter thread by Angie Hong, a Korean American writer, liturgist, and musician, went viral when she wrote about the racial slurs her kids had experienced, and the conversations she's had with her kids about them. I reached out and asked if she'd be willing to talk more, and she graciously accepted.[21]

Angie shared that she tweeted that short thread in a state of exhaustion and overwhelm over her kids' experiences of racial slurs. Her kids were starting to normalize the comments to the point that it was no big deal to them anymore. The comments they experienced surfaced Angie's own memories of being bullied, such as when a group of blond cheerleaders cornered her in a bathroom in high school in North Carolina, spewing racial slurs in her face.

In her attempt to help equip her boys, ages nine and twelve, with tools on how to handle racial slurs, Angie was not intending for her thread to be prescriptive or go viral, but her tools evidently struck a chord. Here's the Twitter thread, and I share it as quoted because it's a helpful guide for parents, offering potential language to use. Angie models how to empower our kids to make decisions for themselves:[22]

> First, it's not ok when people use racial slurs ("ching chong," etc.) at any time, at any point, even if they're having fun.

> When you hear someone yelling a racial slur, you have a choice. If you decide to confront them, make sure you're in a safe place and there's a trusted teacher or maybe some ally friends, and that they're ACTUALLY allies.

> If you confront someone, first tell them that it's not ok and it's racist. If you want to educate them, be prepared to explain why it's racist and why it will not be tolerated. You may also have to educate your teachers, even if they dismiss you.

> If you have no safety when you confront them, then you either learn to defend yourself if you get attacked, or you must walk away and eventually let go of the racial slur.

> If you're troubled by the racial slur, talk to parents about it. Talk to parents anyways. We will tell you of your preciousness. We will affirm that you were made in God's image, in your particularities. We will remind you that no one can ever change that with racial slurs.

This thread struck a chord with me because I wasn't equipped on how to handle situations like this when I was at that age, and I didn't have the language to offer my kids when they were that age either. Angie said their family had a fruitful conversation and her children asked questions about what to do in varying scenarios. She said their family talks about race-related events when they happen in the news or in school, and these conversations occur anywhere from once or twice a week to once every other week. In other words, it comes up *regularly*.

For many of us, especially if we grew up with immigrant parents, we might not have grown up having these conversations. Dear BIPOC friends, if this is the case, it's time to talk about it. Black families have had no choice but to have conversations like these for years. Race conversations are becoming more normalized, and according to Esau McCaulley, the topic of race flows in and out of conversation with his Black friends regularly.[23] But, if you have not talked about it yet, it's not too late to start.

Angie shared that she was talking with her boys in the car about questions others were asking them, such as, "Are you Japanese? Are you Chinese?" (Yes, this is the "So, what are you?" question yet again!) Angie pointed out that when Jesus was asked similar kinds of questions about his ministry and his identity, his answers were confounding and bizarre, sometimes making no sense. Sometimes he even answered back with a question. Angie gave her sons the suggestion to "confound" others, too, with statements like "I was born in Durham. I'm American. Where were you born?" When she took her boys to a Lunar New Year festival in their city recently, her youngest son said, "I liked going to that place because I can see who I am."[24]

Parents, aunties, guardians, caregivers, let's remind our kids who they are: they are beautiful and made in God's image. There is no one solution for all of our scenarios, but as trusted caregivers, we must be having conversations with our children. Let's listen, discuss, offer tools, guidance, and our support. Give your children space to talk it through. Offer them ideas of how they can choose to respond. Let them know you are a safe space to process these experiences. If this is new for you, it's okay to start now. Normalize having these conversations with your children. Let's remind our kids of the loving affirmation that they are precious and made in God's image, and they are loved unconditionally. Can we ever tell them they are loved enough?

## ADOPTEES AND LONELINESS

Transracial adoptees (adoptees of color in white families) may reflect back that their white parents didn't fully understand what it was like to be a child of a different color than themselves. The adoptee's experience in the world is different from that of their parents, and they may feel like a "racial impostor," such as a Black child growing up in a white family who feels disconnected from Black culture. Some adoptees experience what's called *transracial adoptee paradox*, in which they experience the privilege of growing up with whiteness and then when they leave, they find themselves suddenly facing the realities of being a racial minority.[25]

Lily was six months old when she was adopted from China into a white American family in the Midwest. She struggled as a child and never felt like she belonged. Academically she felt challenged, and she knew early on that she was different from her peers. She was surrounded by a white majority and found herself doing anything she could to fit in. After high school, she began dying her hair and tried to hide the fact that she was an Asian American woman. She made decisions that came from a place of not knowing who she was (beloved), or who God was. Her choices led her down a dark path to despair, heartache, and loss. It was not until her late twenties that she began to feel the pursuit of God, and in that pursuit, she began to walk away from her old life. Her heart softened toward her adoption, and she began to embrace who she was. Today, she is serving in an online Asian American women's ministry and her church. She has found community, joy, and healing, and each day is leaning more and more into her true identity.

## KNOWING OUR NAMES

"Could you spell that?"[26]

I've been asked countless times to spell my name. Almost every week, in fact, I'm asked to spell or pronounce my name. For years, I lamented that I lacked a simple American nickname to make this part of life easier for us all. When I was younger, I imagined having a simple, easy-to-pronounce, no-one-would-ever-stumble-over name. I imagined a teacher calling my very ordinary name during attendance on the first day of class and moving immediately to the next student.

In later years, I imagined golden moments of introductions where others would shake my hand, say my very ordinary name, and simply move on in the conversation. I wouldn't be asked for a repeat, or a spelling, with all eyes focused on me for an answer.

I wondered if it would help to have a name that sounds like everyone else's. I thought a simple name would remove a barrier—a big one—between us. I couldn't change my skin color, which was Big Barrier #1. But I could change my name, which felt like Big Barrier #2. Maybe a simple, American name would make it easier for others to talk to me. Jhumpa Lahiri, in the novel *The Namesake*, writes, "How many times does a person write his name in a lifetime—a million? Two million?"[27] Indeed, if I had a dollar for how many times I've had to spell and pronounce my name, I could buy myself multiple round-trip flights to India and any other country I wanted to visit.

Sometimes I hear unspoken thoughts such as: *yes, go ahead and change your name. You're in* my *country now. You're in America.* It's not uncommon for "foreigners" to adopt American nicknames. I've had people ask me to choose a nickname (or arbitrarily assign one) because they did not want to say my name. I've seen some funny jokes on the internet about substituting short, cute American nicknames for long Indian ones. I've even laughed at those jokes. My ethnic name fits those stereotypes, and for a time at least, the idea made some sense to me.

It made sense, that is, until I overheard an Indian friend talking about one of her other Indian friends who had adopted an American name. "Traitor," she chuckled, referring to her friend's decision to adopt an American name. She was half joking, but when I heard the word *traitor*, I felt, once again, stuck in the middle of two places. I thought a nickname would make things easier and help bridge an ethnic gap, but if I made my name more palatable to European Americans, I could be considered a traitor by fellow Indian Americans. There is no name for this in-between place. Those of us who are immigrants, refugees, or who possess ethnic names in American culture walk in this in-between land of "So What Do We Call Ourselves?"

Some folks talk about "living in the hyphen," the space of the both/and identity. In 2021, the *New York Times* dropped the hyphen in "Asian American." The hyphen suggests "otherness," being part American but not fully American because of ethnic identity. Dropping the hyphen between Indian and American, for example, suggests "Indian" to be an adjective, as in a *type* of American.[28]

With four in ten Americans identifying as nonwhite, our names are changing. Linguist Katherine He studied census data of 348 million American baby names from 1880 to 2017. She found that boys are four times more likely to have a "unique" name, and girls are three times as likely to have a "unique" name, with "unique" equating to "nonwhite." Sometimes a global event, such as 9/11, or crimes targeted against Asians, can spur us on a journey to reclaim our ethnic names and our identities (and hence choose cultural or ethnic names).[29] On the other hand, such events also call unwanted attention to those of us with foreign-sounding names as our ethnicities are thrust into the spotlight.

Names are part of our cultural identity. Other cultures have naming traditions or customs that confer meaning or a sense of ancestral respect.[30] In some Asian cultures, the family name comes first, followed by a generation name, and the individual's personal name is given last—a concept that is foreign to most Americans. In Spanish and Latin American cultures, both the mother's and father's surnames are given to children.

"Names provide us an opportunity for agency that can lead to life, death, repentance, or love,"[31] explain the authors of *Learning Our Names*. When others say my name and spell it correctly, they are essentially saying, *I see you. I respect you. Your name is different, but you don't have to change your name for me. Just be who you are. I'll meet you there.* They are telling me they *see* me. We value other human beings when we refer to them by name, when we make an effort to spell and pronounce their name as close to the desired way as possible. Getting to know me means learning my name. It has taken years for *me* to get used to my own ethnic name in the cultural context of living in the United States—and the process of doing so has been teaching and healing for me. The story of our names is, in a sense, the story of ourselves.

In the anonymous text *The Cloud of Unknowing*, we read that "this desire to be loved for who we are, for our self alone, is a mirror or reflection of how God loves us. And, therefore, when we raise ourselves up to love, we enter the deep dimension of the inner life."[32] It is a challenging wound to heal and difficult to live fully integrated selves and lives when society-at-large rejects or minimizes our name, personhood, reality, experience, and existence.

• • •

In the science lesson I discussed where the only color visible is the one *not* absorbed by an object, we learn that the physics behind color itself is a multidimensional story. If color is a wavelength of light, then white is actually not a color on the visible light spectrum. When we see white, we are seeing *all* the colors bouncing off the object and hitting our eyes.

For objects that appear black to our eyes, we are seeing the color black because all the colors are absorbed by the object—nothing is reflected back for us to see. That's why darkness looks black: there is nothing for us to look at.

It is curious that humans chose these two "non-colors" to describe color in each other. The physics behind the colors themselves is representative of what has taken place in our world, and how people of color from the African continent became referred to as "Black," as if they were seen as nonexistent, nonentities. Colonizers and slave handlers erased their humanity by treating them as slaves and subjugating them. That is how many have chosen to "see" Black folks: not worthy, less-than, dehumanized. Additionally, the racial divide is often defined by this Black-white binary, yet there is so much more to be known, so many colors in-between.

• • •

## EL ROI

Imagine having a name that meant "Foreign Thing." Unthinkable, right? Yet, that is the approximate translation of *Hagar*, the name of Sarah's handmaiden.[33] Sarah was married to Abraham, but in the story, Sarah gave Hagar to Abraham because Sarah and Abraham had no children. Hagar then gave birth to Ishmael. But Hagar's name, which isn't really a name, means something like "foreign thing." And this is exactly how she was treated. Not as a person with autonomy, but as a slave, an object to be used at will. When Hagar was forced out of Abraham's household, God met her in the desert, told her to return to the household, and declared that her son should be named *Ishmael*, which means "God hears" (Gen 16:11). Hagar responds by naming God *El Roi*, which means "the God Who Sees." The "Foreign Thing" was seen, heard, and known.

Though we may walk through life unknown by society at-large or in majority white spaces, we are known by the Creator. Being known necessitates a curiosity beyond stereotypes and toward specifics. Being known means we are known completely and loved by a Creator who sees the good, the bad, and the ugly and loves us anyway.

Indeed, we have a God who sees us and knows us. We are not foreign things but beloved people, those who belong. We are seen, heard, known, loved, and embraced. And if culture at-large doesn't see us or know us for who we are, we can be certain that God does and will not stay silent forever. We are not isolated or forgotten. We are seen, and as we negotiate belonging and assimilation, we are integrated into the story of humanity, and a story of love and belonging crafted by a God who sees.

## SO, WHAT ARE YOU?

God knows your name
Your past, present, future

You are seen, remembered, known
In the land you are looking for
You belong both/and
There is no either/or
You are known
And loved as-is
You are not out here
Making it all alone

## QUESTIONS FOR REFLECTION
## AND DISCUSSION

1. In what ways have you experienced belonging "as-is"? Describe these experiences in a journal or small group.

2. Writing prompts:
   - "What I wish others knew about me is . . ."
   - "I feel isolated when . . ."

3. Do you have a name story? Take some time to journal or share in a small group.

4. What strategies have you used to cope or adapt to the dominant culture around you? Journal or share in a small group.

# 5

# MARGINALIZED AND STRANDED

*My humanity is bound up in yours,*
*for we can only be human together.*

DESMOND TUTU

Years ago, I had a coworker, a lively and funny gal, who once made a comment about someone she knew who had jet black hair, blue eyes, and white porcelain skin, and how perfect and beautiful that combination was. She said this while glancing over at me. It was a jab, because I possessed the black hair but none of the other features. She was insinuating I was inferior to this majestic creature she was describing. But what does one do in that situation, or at least, what did I do? I pretended it meant nothing and continued on as if it were all normal, as did everyone else at the table. I wondered if any of my all-white coworkers noticed that barb. Was it intentional?

## UNCONSCIOUS BIAS

This is an example of a microaggression, one of those types of comments that come at people of color regularly, daily sometimes, one of those "thousand little cuts." Sometimes microaggressions are direct, sometimes they are sideways insults.

Part of the frustration we experience is the roadblock we face when other folks believe they (or others) do not have bias or prejudice against people of color. The fact is that all of us do have what is called "unconscious bias." Even people of color have unconscious bias. Biases appear in the form of prejudices, discrimination, microaggressions, and macroaggressions—all sentiments and actions that result from othering. It can be hard to recognize unconscious bias in ourselves without a little help. There are tests that help us uncover our unconscious biases for or against certain groups and ethnicities. After taking these assessments, almost all of us walk away having learned something new about ourselves and how we view others.

This was my experience when I took a test. The purpose of these courses and tests is not to shame but to expose those hidden biases we are unaware of and help us understand how they manifest in our daily lives and decision-making. (A free test is available through Project Implicit.[1]) I think most people genuinely want to know what biases they have. Many people I've talked to are fearful of hurting someone else's feelings, so they say and do nothing. Knowing our biases helps us overcome that inertia so we are more self-aware.

The Othering & Belonging Institute in California states, "Othering is the problem of our time. Belonging is the solution." They offer curriculum, case studies, workshops, and podcasts with resources on belonging, as well as a network of social justice activists, policymakers, leaders, and academics, all with the goal of transformative change in areas including housing, disability, food systems, race, health, and the arts. The Othering & Belonging Institute describes belonging as "having a meaningful voice and the opportunity to participate in the design of political, social, and cultural structures that shape one's life—the right to both contribute and make demands upon society and political institutions."[2]

Othering is the problem of our time, scrolling is our dominant activity, and loneliness is the condition of our present age. Belonging is having a voice.

## REPRESENTATION

When I was twelve, I secretly wanted to be in show business. I knew it would never happen for me, but I enjoyed participating in a creative drama group in college and even performed in a few community productions as an adult. I wholeheartedly applaud and support those who perform, sing, dance, and act, and especially those who are breaking stereotypes and representing their communities. This is why when I was in New York not too long ago, I made time to attend the musicals *Aladdin* and *Hamilton*, because both shows have diverse casts. Both shows were outstanding and excellent. It's exciting to see these new efforts toward more diverse casts and stories.

Some other recent positive strides have been made in media representation. The movie *Everything Everywhere All at Once*, which was unapologetically Asian, made history by winning seven Oscars. The year 2023 had the highest number of Asian Americans nominated for Oscars ever (with only twenty-three nominees in Oscar history). *Shang-Chi & the Legend of the Ten Rings* starred an Asian Canadian in the lead. *Ms. Marvel* was another steppingstone in Asian representation with a South Asian Canadian in the lead role, and it's also fascinating they included the historical event of the Partition of India in the storyline.

A few Asians here and there, however, aren't representative of all of Asia. At a recent gathering I attended with AAPI leaders, pastors, and thinkers in Chicago, a Filipino man shared there is a vacuous hole of Filipino representation in the United States. Lea Salonga, the Filipina singer who sang for Disney (songs such as "A

Whole New World"), is the only Filipina representative for their community on the national level, and it was only twenty years later, after the internet, when we finally saw her face. More recently, the film *Easter Sunday* was hailed as a milestone for Filipino representation in film.[3] But Filipinos often are left out of conversations and representation—even though Filipinos make up nearly 20 percent of the Asian population in the United States.

In another example, Angelo Quinto was a thirty-year-old Filipino Navy veteran in California who was experiencing a mental health crisis. Police officers responded to a call, and an officer put his knee on Quinto's neck for five minutes. Quinto died three days later. This happened in 2021, after the death of George Floyd, who died in a similar manner. But news outlets left out the fact that Quinto was an Asian American man. Quinto's ethnic identity was erased. There were massive protests all over the United States after Floyd's death, yet the name of Angelo Quinto remains relatively unknown, and there were no charges against the officers in Quinto's case.[4] The lack of acknowledgment of ethnic identity amplifies the loneliness, adding to trauma by erasure.

A similar note can be added about the Hmong and Native American populations, which also suffer from a lack of representation. Likewise, African Americans represent nearly 13 percent of cable shows, which is approximately the same percentage in the population, but only 6 percent are writers, directors, or producers. Despite making up 19 percent of the population of the United States, Latinos are also grossly misrepresented or underrepresented in the media as well.[5]

The media and movie industry continue to favor white leads, while demographic trends suggest nonwhite populations are bigger consumers of media. According to media expert and sociologist Nancy Wang Yuen:

In fact, people of color are the biggest media consumers—exceeding white audiences. In 2014, people of color purchased 44 percent of domestically sold movie tickets. African Americans watch more television than does any other racial group: nearly 200 hours per month, or roughly 60 more hours than the total audience, according to Nielsen. Latinos are more likely than any other ethnic group to go to movies and are growing in their annual ticket purchases.[6]

According to a report issued by PEN America, the book publishing industry is disproportionately white, too. Ninety-five percent of American fiction books published between 1950 and 2018 were written by white people, although the United States is made up of 42 percent people of color, and 25 percent of America's adult readers are people of color. There have been diversity, equity, and inclusion efforts in publishing but it's usually cyclical and transient. Some efforts on social media have tried to bring awareness of the issue, with hashtags such as #WeNeedDiverseBooks, a reaction to an all-white and all-male panel of authors at a BookCon gathering. In addition, the hashtag #PublishingPaidMe was used to expose inequities in book advances.[7]

The danger of not acknowledging the diversity of audiences in media and publishing is that we are not "seeing one another" in a multitude of ways. The expression "out of sight, out of mind" leads to invisibility. Our busy and self-absorbed culture is designed to foster an attitude of indifference. "Indifference," writes O'Donohue, "is one of the hallmarks of our times. It is said that indifference is necessary for power; to hold control one has to be successfully indifferent to the needs and vulnerabilities of those under control."[8] Stereotypes and lack of representation are contributing factors that lead to indifference. Indifference is isolating. Indifference contributes to loneliness. And these experiences lead to feelings of being stranded.

"If we are to have peace on earth, our loyalties must become ecumenical rather than sectional. Our loyalties must transcend our race, our tribe, our class, and our nation. . . . We must either learn to live together as brothers [and sisters] or we are all going to perish together as fools," said Martin Luther King Jr.[9] Modern exile (or isolation) for the person of color is being relegated to the outside, reduced to a stereotype, being known only as a one-dimensional character, a singular narrative.

## INSTITUTIONS AND ETHNIC LONELINESS

Our organizations, institutions, churches, and systems can inadvertently or deliberately contribute to the perpetuation of ethnic loneliness. It happens through policies, regulations, organizational structures, cultural norms, and other ways. These can result in the following:

- *Lack of diversity and representation.* Organizations that lack diversity in leadership can create environments where minority groups feel invisible and underrepresented. The absence of relatable role models and mentors can contribute to a sense of isolation.

- *Cultural insensitivity.* Systems that are not culturally sensitive can isolate marginalized individuals by failing to recognize and accommodate diverse cultural practices, values, and beliefs, leading to alienation and exclusion.

- *Discriminatory policies.* Policies that discriminate against certain ethnic groups or favor others can create a hostile environment and perpetuate feelings of isolation and injustice.

- *Microaggressions and bias.* Not addressing microaggressions, stereotypes, and biases allows these behaviors to persist, leading to hostile and unwelcoming environments.

- *Lack of access to resources.* Systems that limit access to resources, opportunities, education, and health care based on ethnicity lead to unequal treatment and amplify exclusion.
- *Language barriers.* Organizations that do not provide language support or accessible communication can isolate individuals who struggle to navigate systems due to language differences.
- *Tokenism.* When institutions use diversity images in media to appear inclusive without making substantial changes, it leads to feelings of being used.
- *Segregation.* Segregation of minority groups into specific neighborhoods or institutions can lead to social isolation and limit opportunities for interaction with others in the wider community, as well as access to resources.
- *Inclusive programming.* Not prioritizing or funding programs that celebrate diversity or promote cross cultural understanding leads to alienation and perpetuates ethnic loneliness.
- *Racial profiling.* Being targeted by law enforcement or security personnel based on racial or ethnic characteristics, resulting in unjust treatment, leads to fear, stress, mental anguish, isolation, and loneliness.

Addressing the specific roles our institutions, organizations, and systems have in perpetuating ethnic loneliness requires a commitment to structural change and to cultural sensitivity. It involves commitment from leadership and implementing policies that promote diversity and inclusion, addressing biases and stereotypes, providing accessible resources, and fostering environments where individuals from all ethnic backgrounds feel valued and heard.

In education, it might require including curriculum that is culturally relevant and includes histories of minority students. It means hiring a diverse teaching team and providing mentors who can be positive role models to minority students. It involves addressing language differences, which can create barriers for children who are nonnative speakers, affecting their comprehension and academic performance. It might involve having holidays that celebrate different cultures. Furthermore it would involve ensuring adequate funding and resources for schools that serve marginalized communities.

In health care, it might involve addressing the disparities that minority groups experience due to limited access to quality care and preventive services. Language barriers can hinder communication between patients and providers, leading to misunderstandings and misdiagnoses. Cultural competency training can help health care providers in understanding that some groups fear stigma or discrimination by seeking care, particularly for sensitive health issues. Lack of insurance coverage, high health care costs, and limited access to affordable care can prevent marginalized groups from seeking care. Moreover, limited health literacy can make it difficult for individuals to understand medical information and make informed decisions about their health.

In employment, bias and discrimination during the hiring process can prevent qualified individuals from obtaining jobs. A lack of representation in leadership positions can limit career advancement, and negative assumptions and microaggressions in the workplace can create a hostile environment and limit career growth. Furthermore, pay disparities based on gender, race, or ethnicity can contribute to financial insecurity and limit economic mobility.

In the legal system, minority individuals may be disproportionately targeted by law enforcement due to racial profiling. Further, many marginalized individuals lack access to quality legal representation, which can lead to unequal outcomes in the justice system. Limited language support comes into play here as well, as it can hinder understanding and participation in legal proceedings. And finally, implicit bias within the legal system can lead to unfair treatment and sentencing for individuals from minority backgrounds.

Addressing these barriers would require concerted efforts at multiple levels, involving policy changes, cultural competency training, increased representation, and raising awareness about systemic inequalities.

## LIVING A BOTH/AND EXISTENCE

Several respondents of the survey I conducted indicated they felt alienated in their white church spaces. A few others responded they felt this way in other predominantly white spaces as well, including in their workplace and at school, either as a student or as a teacher or parent. Some respondents even said they felt alone among their own ethnic group. A Korean American respondent said she feels most welcome in spaces where people of color, and especially women of color, are welcomed. She added that even among people of color, patriarchy is still a barrier for her in interacting with men of color, who can wield power in oppressive ways.

In our racial and ethnic identities, we can find both meaning and belonging, but also marginalization and disbelonging. We experience the tension of living in "both/and." We live with the traditions and stories of our unique ethnic and racial identities while simultaneously participating in the larger dominant culture. We live in a place that sometimes tells us to leave, and regularly informs us we are not welcome, while we attempt to build our homes here. Our country tells us we can sometimes belong and yet do not belong. Sometimes we are defined using economic language, such as being described as assets or liabilities, reducing us to commodities and terms used for products and services. But this place of both belonging and disbelonging is a place of tension and growth. In the ache of disbelonging, we also find the beauty of belonging. It is a both/and.

In this both/and existence, we live in the tension of joy and sorrow, life and death. We live in a paradox, according to author Marlena Graves, where "the way up is down."[10] The last will be made first (Mt 19:30), to live we must die (Mt 16:25), weakness is where we find strength (2 Cor 12:10), and we gain by losing (Phil 3:7-8). What does this mean for the ethnic minority and what does it mean for ethnic loneliness? Perhaps it suggests our very hope and healing come from the places we least expect: from the margins of our lives, from the places and identities pushed to the edges. Perhaps "there are years that ask questions, and years that answer," as author Zora Neale Hurston wrote, and we'll find answers as we travel the path of loneliness.

## WOMEN OF COLOR AND DOMESTIC VIOLENCE

Some years ago, I went to a party, which was at a Hindu temple, and I saw papers taped to the walls with a message that read something like this: "If you aren't safe, if he's hitting you, call didi" with a phone number to call (*didi* means "sister" in Hindi). In traditional Indian culture, as a woman, you're taught that you leave your family of origin after marriage, and you belong to your husband's family. In some families, even in cases of domestic violence, the woman's family will not take her back even if she must flee for her safety. More often than not, heads turn the other way, and women are expected to stay and make the best of it, with others not wishing to interfere. Divorce is taboo (though society is changing). When it comes to the issue of domestic violence, in regard to honor/shame cultures, there is a strong sense of secrecy, patriarchy, and protecting the family name and reputation, making it much more difficult for a woman of color to leave her situation. She also may be bound financially and unable to find another option with no other support system.

In 2022, a twenty-nine-year-old Pakistani American woman in Chicago was murdered by her ex-husband after she opened up on social media about the stigma of being a South Asian divorced woman. This was 2022 and in the United States. The values of male supremacy and patriarchy follow immigrants to other countries.[11] This is of course not just true in Pakistan, but other countries also, such as India, Afghanistan, and others.

The majority of the world's poor are women,[12] and women of color are disproportionately affected by domestic partner/intimate partner violence. The United Nations calls it a major public health problem:[13]

- Violence against women—particularly intimate partner violence and sexual violence—is a major public health problem and a violation of women's human rights.

- Estimates published by WHO indicate that globally about 1 in 3 (30%) women worldwide have been subjected to either physical and/or sexual intimate partner violence or non-partner sexual violence in their lifetime.

One-third of women affected by physical violence globally is unacceptable. According to the Asian Pacific Institute on Gender-Based Violence, between 21 and 55 percent of Asian women in the United States report experiencing intimate physical and/or sexual violence during their lifetimes. Twenty-four percent of Asian women report being stalked in their lifetimes.[14] The pandemic resulted in a surge in domestic violence calls by Asian American women, who often don't report abuse, because of strong pressure to conceal abuse, and also concern about risks of deportation, anti-Asian racism, and financial instability.[15] Minority women living with domestic abuse experience another level of isolation and loneliness.

Non-Hispanic Black and American Indian/Alaska Native women experienced the highest rates of homicide.[16] American Indian and Alaska Native women experience assault and domestic violence more than any other ethnicity, and over 84 percent of Native women experience assault during their lifetimes. In addition, "on some reservations in the United States, the murder rate of Native women is 10 times higher than in the rest of the nation. American Indian/Alaska Native children experience PTSD at the same rate as combat veterans from the Iraq and Afghanistan wars."[17] The PTSD of Native children is the same as war veterans.

In the Black community,[18]

- 45 percent of Black women have experienced intimate partner physical violence, intimate partner sexual violence, and/or intimate partner stalking in their lifetimes.

- An estimated 51 percent of Black adult female homicides are related to intimate partner violence.

As I read all these statistics, it's hard to hold back the emotion. Perhaps you feel the same. BIPOC women are isolated, living with the taboo and shame of domestic violence, experiencing a deep isolation, and feel lonely and stranded to another degree.

## LEARNING

Despite my experiences growing up in Alabama, I had some of my own reckoning to do when it came to understanding and acknowledging ethnic loneliness and systemic racism. For years, I did not acknowledge or understand the systemic racism that I now see visible in our society. I thought reports were exaggerated, or I denied it, and I was unwilling to engage the idea they might be true. But gradually I was convicted that I had not read or heard the points of view from those who were saying it was true. I had focused on my own viewpoint and believed corroborating narratives, without doing my own homework. I hadn't acknowledged the sin of racism in my own life. I knew that the work of other sin in my life was ongoing (such as selfishness, impatience, covetousness). Why did I think I was exempt from this one?

During the years I served as a high school debate coach, I learned (and taught) that we need to see all sides of an argument. The best debaters can defend both positions well. This entails learning both sides of an issue deeply, including those viewpoints we disagree with or don't fully understand. This perspective, alongside current events such as the embroiled political election of 2016, the killing of George Floyd, and my own identity journey, contributed to helping me realize I wasn't seeing all sides of the issue when it came to systemic and structural inequalities. I could agree that there was racism in some individual cases, but I didn't see it as a systemic or structural problem. I had not put into practice the idea of learning all sides of an issue when it came to understanding racial divisions. I believed one side: my own side. I realized I needed to be a fair judge on this issue of race and systemic racism—even though I personally had my own stories of racism to share. So, I read books, listened to interviews and podcasts, and heard voices that I had previously dismissed. I began to think, pray, and grow in my understanding of the other side of the argument. I knew, in my heart, I had been wrong in the assumptions I had personally made about racism. My assimilation and proximity to white culture meant that I had absorbed the narratives I had been told about Black and white people. I began to see the systemic structures we have in our society that have created a divide and disadvantages to Black, Indigenous, Asian, and other marginalized groups in our population.

What implications did this change have on me? It meant I couldn't agree with certain views I once believed. It meant I would continue listening and learning. It meant that my silence could also mean complicity. I had to ask myself how and when I would add my voice to these issues. It was, I confess, kind of scary. I realized I had been comfortable and complacent—I was hiding, which was a privilege, and though I had stories of my own to tell, I had not had to confront the issues others had no choice but to confront on a daily basis.

At the same time, I admit, I wanted to distance myself from the label of "Christian" as I became more and more embarrassed by the behavior and attitudes publicly displayed by some Christians. I didn't want to be associated with bigotry and hatred—which became the overarching narrative about Christians and their actions, particularly regarding the 2016 political election and in other issues as well. I was more than embarrassed. I was disappointed, angry, confused, and frustrated. I was compelled to self-reflect: just exactly who was I now? What was I? Where was Jesus in all this? It felt like he had been lost. I felt lost. Once I stopped to think about it, I realized I had internalized certain narratives about myself and others, and held various assumptions (and this is work I am still doing in my own life), but that was the start. I committed to know, understand, and own my own ethnic identity; it was paramount to my own healing and sense of belonging. Dietrich Bonhoeffer died in a concentration camp in 1945 but while imprisoned, he wrote a poem called "Who Am I?" where he attempts to answer the question of who he is:

Who am I? This or the Other?
Am I one person today and tomorrow another?
Am I both at once? A hypocrite before others,
And before myself a contemptible woebegone weakling?
Or is something within me still like a beaten army

Fleeing in disorder from victory already achieved?
Who am I? They mock me, these lonely questions of mine.
Whoever I am, Thou knowest, O God, I am thine![19]

I don't have the answers to all of my questions. I'm still searching. In the midst of unknowing and uncertainty and this unmooring, these words help: "For he himself is our peace, who has made the two groups one and has destroyed the barrier, the dividing wall of hostility" (Eph 2:14). As those who have been reconciled with God, the church should understand what reconciliation looks like and model reconciliation, the inclusion of all ethnicities, for us. John describes a vision he had: "After this I looked, and there before me was a great multitude that no one could count, from every nation, tribe, people and language, standing before the throne and before the Lamb" (Rev 7:9). This vison represents God's dream of a future, which is a multiethnic one—not a monoethnic one.

When Christ lived on earth, he did not seek company only with those who were just like himself, hanging out only with the hometown boys from the provincial town of Nazareth ("Nazareth! Can anything good come from there?" Jn 1:46), or from Joseph's hometown of Bethlehem, or only with the religious leaders who held the power, or with those who had the loudest voice in the public square. He didn't "assimilate" with the views of the powerful and religious establishment but led with humility and as a servant. In fact, he challenged the religious authorities of his time, sharply criticizing them for their hypocrisy and legalism (Mt 23).

While Jesus did spend time with the "lost sheep of Israel," he also clearly showed his ministry would extend to the Gentiles, even more so after his departure. He went to women, to the lepers, to the tax collectors, to the prostitutes, to those who held the lowest status in society. He practiced empathy. On one occasion, he was leaving Jericho and a huge crowd was following him. Two blind men were sitting by the road and when they heard Jesus was walking by, they cried out to him for mercy. The crowd rebuked them, telling them to be quiet, but Jesus stopped and asked what they wanted. "We want our sight," they answered. Jesus had compassion on them and touched their eyes, and they were healed (Mt 20:29-34). He stopped, he asked, he listened, he acted. In our culture today, the marginalized are also among us: the people of color, the immigrants, the refugees, the elderly, the disabled, and others who are frequently ostracized or demeaned. Seems like this might be a good four-step plan for us to practice too.

## SO, WHAT ARE YOU?

You are a brother
You are a sister
You are familia
We are walking together
On this journey
Of being human
You are perpetually known
You are perpetually wanted
Perpetually foreign, you are not—
Perpetually loved—this is your lot
Your trauma and pain
Are not final
And can be transformed
For burdens of joy

## QUESTIONS FOR REFLECTION AND DISCUSSION

1. Think about occasions when you did and did not feel marginalized. What circumstances or situation existed at that

time? What factors are within your control to change, and which ones are beyond your control?

2. Writing prompts:

- "I long to be represented in . . ."
- "The biggest area of change I want to see in my community/church/organization/workplace/school is . . ."

3. In what ways do you live a both/and existence?

4. What areas of learning do you feel you need in your life? What specific change would you like to see to bring the dream of Revelation 7:9 closer to a living reality? Spend some time journaling and praying.

# 6

# EXILED AND DISCONNECTED

*Without knowing what I am*
*and why I am here, life is impossible.*

LEO TOLSTOY

*How can you draw close to God*
*when you are far from your own self?*

AUGUSTINE, *CONFESSIONS*

I was sitting on the bleachers in the high school gym studying for my Spanish quiz. I think I was in seventh grade. A group of boys I didn't know were sitting a few rows behind me, talking about me. I don't think they knew I could hear their conversation.

"I think she's Black."

"No, she's not Black. I think she's Hawaiian."

"What is she?"

They didn't get the right answer, and I pretended I couldn't hear. For all I know, they may still be trying to figure it out.

But to be honest, they raised a question I had trouble answering myself. Answering "So, what are you?" isn't so simple. Sometimes it's clear my answer doesn't give the person what they seek. If I say I'm from Alabama, they pause and wait for more. "No, I mean where are you from, *really*? Before Alabama?" Or they try this tactic: "Where are your parents from?" To continually be asked this question is a sign that one is a "perpetual foreigner."

Unfortunately, one way that people try to create a sense of belonging is by *othering* other members of a group. Setting up a line between "us" and "them" makes the sense of belonging stronger with the "us." To be a perpetual foreigner, to be othered, or marginalized, creates a sense of "belonging uncertainty," a feeling that our belonging is always up for negotiation, and never final, and this is particularly true for minority and underrepresented populations.[1]

Our individualistic society and increasing reliance on digital technologies to communicate present a burden for the ethnic minority in particular. With a lack of embodied presence with one another, we are more likely to misunderstand, alienate, isolate, and even hate those who are not like us. But within these places of disconnection and exile, we find that our in-between places are actually places with tremendous creativity, power, and resilience.

## INDIVIDUALIST VERSUS COLLECTIVIST CULTURES

Our culture in the United States has become more individualistic over the years. We operate more and more alone with less reliance and need for others. We have more self-checkout lanes, drive-throughs, doorstep delivery, personal playground equipment for our yards, personal entertainment devices, and the list goes on. This has implications on how we view ourselves and our roles in society. With the rise of individualism, we have also seen a decline in participation in traditional institutions such as churches and community organizations. There is an emphasis on autonomy, competition, and independence.

Collectivist cultures, on the other hand, emphasize group harmony, interdependence, social relationships, collective decision-making (soliciting the input of family members or community elders), a sense of group identity (individuals derive a significant part of their identity from their group affiliations), shared responsibility (shared obligations in caregiving for the elderly, supporting relatives, contributing in communal events), and finally, conformity (an expectation to conform to societal norms and expectations to maintain group cohesion).

Pros and cons exist for both individualist and collectivist cultures or societies, of course. If only we could take the best of both! But for the ethnic and racial minority, especially those who come from strong collectivist cultures, these two different values can frequently conflict with one another.

## SOCIAL ISOLATION

It's delightful to watch babies interact with their parents, mimicking their parents' facial expressions and repeating words they have heard. Researchers have found if a parent expresses an emotion, the same neurons fire in that child's brain, mirroring the emotions of the parent. These are called mirror neurons.[2] The matching of behavior, affective states, and biological rhythms between parent and child is called bio-behavioral synchrony, and this lays the foundation from which empathy and our ability to connect with others emerge.[3] Researchers have also observed that monkeys will mirror each other—when a monkey eats a banana, for example, the same neurons fire in the monkey eating the banana as in the monkeys *watching*. Mirroring is a powerful nonverbal tool, and when done well, mirroring can earn waiters higher tips, result in higher sales, and even help people get dates.[4]

When we do not share the same physical space, we cannot mirror each other, practice eye contact, and understand nuance and tone in conversation. We do not have the opportunity to learn how to visibly respond to facial cues, gestures, subtleties in language, and otherwise interact in deep, meaningful ways. This is critical when we are talking about isolation in general, but it profoundly affects how different ethnic and racial groups communicate. Less interpersonal interaction translates into not only a greater likelihood of misunderstandings but also a greater sense of loneliness, isolation, and fear, especially among those who do not look like us.

Social anxiety is an enduring consequence of the Covid-19 pandemic, which means we are operating with significant relational deficits.[5] When we are not interacting in person, engaging, or mirroring, our avoidance of each other leads to disconnectedness.[6] Disconnectedness leads to distrust, fear, negative beliefs about one another, hatred, and greater polarization. We are hardwired for connection and the results of disconnection are devastating, so we grow even further and further apart. With a dearth of ethnic and racial minority groups interacting with one another and with the white population, we have scant opportunities for deep and meaningful interaction and engagement with one another.

## EXILE

Throughout history, we have employed exile as one of the worst punishments. It was one of the first punishments incurred on humankind, and we have been replicating that punishment on others ever since, including shunning and casting people out of community. Even young children have learned that exclusion is one way to hurt another. People of all ages form cliques and exclude others.

As ethnic minorities, we know the sting of being "othered" because of our racial or ethnic identity. Exile is punishment. We are living in exile from each other, in segregated neighborhoods, in isolated islands behind our screens, and divided by racial and ethnic lines. We experience disbelonging in various spheres: spiritually, geographically, physically, relationally, socially, emotionally, ethnically, racially. Segregation, marginalization, isolation, being othered, and disbelonging are all forms of separation and exile.

We experience the ache of loneliness, the ache of ethnic loneliness in particular, as a sign that something is amiss. As C. S. Lewis observed, "Pain insists upon being attended to. God whispers to us in our pleasures, speaks in our consciences, but shouts in our pains. It is his megaphone to rouse a deaf world."[7] In our present age, loneliness is shouting.

One thing is for certain: we can't navigate through the wilderness of exile and loneliness alone. Cain responded to God's search for Abel by asking, "Am I my brother's keeper?" (Gen 4:9). Today, we are still asking that question (directly or indirectly), as evidenced by our diminishing trust in our neighbor and trends toward social disconnection. Loneliness is so extreme in our neighborhoods that many of us do not even know who our actual neighbors are.[8] We close our doors, flip on the television, scroll on our phones, and continue on with overloaded and busy schedules. We have little interaction with those on our own street. We are suffering silently of loneliness and—like another silent killer, heart disease—our hearts are slowly, quietly being broken.

## HYPERINDIVIDUALISM

We live lives of digital distraction, convenience, and technological addiction; we live lives of transactions,[9] and we do so with a hyperindividualistic mindset. Yet, even while we are going about our lives at this frantic and isolated pace, behind screens and with doorstep delivery, we still long to be seen and known. Technology and machines are currently fulfilling our need for acknowledgment of our personhood. We seek reassurance and affirmation through comments and engagement on social media platforms. When "the defining activity of our times is scrolling" and "the defining challenge of our time is anxiety," then "it is no wonder that the defining condition of our time is loneliness and alienation," according to Crouch.[10] And, I would add, that level of loneliness and alienation is multiplied for the person of color who is increasingly not seen or known in a white-majority space.

Due to our lack of embodied engagement (and other reasons), empathy is on the decline and narcissism is on the rise.[11] Younger people are communicating more through technology.[12] Yet research shows having friends from different social groups helps grow empathy (it reduces anxiety and prejudice).[13] Thus, as our society has shifted to individual enclaves, we're also witnessing a decline in empathy.

In our selfie-obsessed, social media world, we decide on an identity and curate images to fit. We all have the tools at our fingertips to project our voices and preferred persona to the world online at any moment of any day. We can air our opinions and grievances and present the best of ourselves. We give the appearance of fulfillment, and busyness is extolled as a virtue. If we aren't busy, are we even important? But, as Alan Noble writes in *You Are Not Your Own*, all of this comes with a cost:

> This burden manifests as a desperate need to justify our lives through identity crafting and expression . . . because everyone else is also working frantically to craft and express their own identity, society becomes a space of vicious competition between individuals vying for attention, meaning, and significance, not unlike the contrived drama of reality TV.[14]

If we are attempting to define our identities on our own, we are dependent on others to recognize the identity we've chosen. And if we only belong to ourselves, then any relationships or ties or belonging to any other people (or to God) is voluntary.[15] Thus, there is no imperative to get to know my neighbor, to go out of my way, to reach beyond myself and be curious about the people around me, because I have decided I do not belong to them and answer to no one but myself. There is also no compulsion to be civil online. And this is contributing to our fractured state of life.

We are addicted to curated disclosure and crafting our presence and brand online, yet we feel incredibly lonely and unseen. We have lost our connection to one another, and we've attached ourselves to our mobile phones as an extra appendage. We have a rent in our souls, and we fill it up with all sorts of temporary measures that do not satisfy our deepest longings. We have forgotten what it means to belong to ourselves, to others, to God. For the ethnic and racial minority who lives in a space that marginalizes his or her experience, this extends the lack of social connection even further and expands the loneliness.

Are we headed to a new age with loneliness as the norm? Pascal noted in *Pensées*, "I have discovered that all the unhappiness of men arises from one single fact, that they cannot stay quietly in their own chamber."[16] Ironically, in a society that is suffering from loneliness, we don't know how to be alone in healthy ways. We're not *really* sitting alone; we're sitting with devices and multiple forms of entertainment and distraction. In our inability to be truly alone and understand the benefits of solitude, and to whom we belong, we are ever more alone. Social scientist Sherry Turkle writes, "The computer offered the illusion of companionship without the demands of friendship. You could interact but never feel vulnerable to another person." We are eloquent online, but it is an edited version, unlike face-to-face, where we stumble over our words and reveal our vulnerabilities.[17] In person, we can't hide, we blunder through awkward conversation, expose our imperfections, and learn how to navigate all the weird and wonderful moments that occur when humans converse and interact. We increasingly don't know what to do with the disconnect we often experience between our highly curated lives and our imperfect, real ones. This is another kind of exile.

All of my life, I've lived in a place where my skin color doesn't match those around me. But even if I were to move where most people's skin color more closely matched my own, I still wouldn't fit in: they'd expect me to think and act like they do, even speak their language—none of which I can do. We'd match on the outside, but that's where it would end. Kat Armas, in *Abuelita Faith*, writes about this exiled identity and how it became a place of shame:

> Indeed, exile is a complex way of life, always lingering in our psyches. But I often wonder how it became a place of shame. Why have we let dominant culture victimize us in our betweenness? Why do many of us feel bad, less-than, plagued by it? Has dominant culture so convinced us that permanence— in location, and belief—is somehow holy? I wonder, what if this exiled identity is an identity in which we are most alive.[18]

Perhaps our betweenness, this exiled identity, is the place we truly begin to live.

## CAMOUFLAGE

Some species of octopuses are masters of camouflage. They can change color and texture. A specific species, called the mimic octopus, is a master shapeshifter and can even change its shape to mimic other sea creatures.[19] It's probably the world's best camouflage artist. Why hasn't Marvel created a sci-fi octopus-type superhero creature with these extraordinary shape-shifting and camouflage capabilities? Having just one of these abilities would transform anyone's life. Both together? That would be a winner.

For the person of color, having these abilities would mean we could transform into any number of different ethnic identities. But alas, we do not possess such abilities and instead we may have built barriers—invisible walls sprouting protective thorns—to keep others from rubbing too close. From the outside it may appear that some of us are managing well as we try to mask or hide, attempt to fit in or assimilate, and thus give up part of our identities. In the United States, the ideal is white, and people of color live with that ideal haunting us, reminding us we don't fit.

Sara, a biracial woman living in Indiana, who is Filipina (from her mother's side) and white (from her father's side), felt the loneliness of disbelonging when she was in high school. She and her friends read magazines and watched TV shows and movies with pop stars, all of whom were white. All of Sara's friends were white as well; she didn't have Filipino friends in her small Midwestern town. Back then, she thought she would never fit the white ideal of beauty because she could never look like those stars they admired. Sara said that as an adult, watching *Never Have I Ever* episodes, in which the main character is an Asian girl, transported her right back to high school. It reminded her of when her friends would go to her house and see how different it was from their stereotypical white American households, such as how in her home they wore slippers inside the house and how they ate rice and spicy food.

For years, I rejected my ethnicity and dreamed I could transition out of my Brown skin and step into a costume of white. In my imagined white world, I wasn't singled out. I was automatically accepted and included. Others looked at white-self me and *knew* me in a way I wasn't known being Brown, where I didn't have to explain myself or attempt to force my way into belonging. I wanted to change my skin color, my hair color, and my name. I fantasized about this white self and imaginary world when I was Brown. My white world was sparkling, gleaming, pristine, *perfect*.

But this world wasn't real. I allowed these hallucinations to eat away at my own flesh, leaving my own true self to disintegrate, and what would be left surely wouldn't be white. I couldn't shed my old skin like a reptile, with a glowing white covering emerging, because in no reality would I ever magically grow white skin, because I'm obviously not a chameleon.

So, I hid my Indian side, idealizing this white girl persona, upset I was the conspicuous anomaly of Brown flesh among a sea of white faces in the rural South. I learned how to shift identities, like a shapeshifter, from Indian to American and back and forth, with one foot in each continent, my heart divided, torn, and splitting through the tug of war as I sought to belong.

Immigrants and people of color must often revert back and forth from one cultural context to another in a balancing act called *code-switching*. People of color change their behavior or speech to be acceptable to the dominant norms. The strategy is considered a survival tactic, a way to fit in and adapt, but it can result in mental exhaustion.[20] We might use particular language or dress or behavior when among our own communities but then "act more white" when in white-majority organizational settings. This bouncing back and forth also contributes to the sense of isolation and feeling "othered."

In tug of war, eventually one side wins and the other side succumbs. I couldn't keep living fractured. One side couldn't fully win, because neither side fully fit. I was too "American" to be truly Indian, which no one could readily see by looking at me, unless they knew me. The Indian side of me is clearly visible to anyone who looks at me, and I look too Indian to be accepted as "American." I remained stuck in a middle space, wondering where I belonged and where the space was for those like me, who felt caught in liminal spaces.

But the truth is, I was, and am, part of both of these worlds, and the two are not mutually exclusive. We can be both, and don't have to give up one to have the other.

## THE MARGINS

Jesus spent time with those who were longing to be seen, those who were unseen by their society. He went out of his way to visit the Samaritan woman who was drawing water at the well in the hottest part of the day, when no one else would be there. He went to see a Samaritan. Samaritans were despised by the Jews, but here is Jesus, who chose that particular time of day, that location, that person, then initiated the conversation and asked her for some water. Would he accept water from the pot of a detested Samaritan woman? Yes, not only would he do so, but he also offered acceptance and inclusion—he offered the woman a place of belonging. Here is Jesus, showing us how to transcend ethnic barriers between two groups who dislike each other. She went out and told everyone else (Jn 4:4-41). And later when Jesus was resurrected, he appeared not to the disciples first but to women, who were second-class citizens. When Jesus was born, God chose shepherds as an unlikely vector to spread the news. The growth of the church came from these unlikely sources. From the margins.

When Jesus withdrew to a "lonely" place, this refers to a physical separation (Luke 5:16). But Jesus was lonely, too, in the sense in which we speak of loneliness today. He was surrounded by people who did not understand him. He was under such immense distress in the Garden of Gethsemane that his sweat was bloody. He was rejected by society, and most of his closest companions deserted him and wrongfully accused him as a criminal. He was nailed to a tree and crucified. The book of Isaiah prophesies, "He was despised and rejected by mankind, a man of suffering, and familiar with pain.

Like one from whom people hide their faces he was despised, and we held him in low esteem" (Is 53:3). If we believe Jesus endured the full gamut of human emotion and experience while living on earth, then he not only experienced loneliness, but he was also intimately acquainted with it. Quite possibly loneliness clung to him closer than any of his warm-blooded human companions. We don't have a God who knows nothing about us; he *was human*. Jesus walked rocky roads full of potholes, he traversed trails of disbelonging just like we do, and experienced abandonment, abuse, pain, grief, rejection, and loneliness.

God is there, in our in-between spaces, in the margins. Where was Jesus constantly going? To the margins, to the people outcast, to those on the bottom, to those forgotten by society. He didn't seek wealth, fame, or power, nor did he coddle the rich, the powerful, the wealthy. He didn't seek to manipulate the masses to gain popularity. Don't lose hope because you are in the margins. It is a place where God dwells.

## SO, WHAT ARE YOU?

You are one of many
Yet you are unique
None created like you
You are one of millions
Who want to be seen and known
And accepted as yourself
In your own skin and culture
You want to belong as yourself
You are not a mistake
We are walking together
On this journey
Of being human

Pick up your identities
Reorder them
And live in harmony
With who you are
Your exile is really
An expansive space
Exemplifying
The beauty and complexity
Of Creator God

## QUESTIONS FOR REFLECTION AND DISCUSSION

1. What about being Black, Brown, Asian, Latino, Hispanic, Mixed, Native, or other ethnicity feeds you? Journal or share in a small group. This might be a list that you keep handy and continue coming back to.

2. Writing prompts:
   - "The characteristics I appreciate about the culture I live in are ..."
   - "The characteristics I want to change about the culture I live in are ..."

3. In what ways have you experienced exile in your life? How can your "in-betweenness" or place of exile be a gift?

4. How has technology affected your sense of belonging? In what ways has technology alleviated, as well as exacerbated, your sense of loneliness? Explain.

# PART TWO

# SO, WHAT CAN BE DONE?

*The Path to Belonging*

# 7

# TRAUMA AND HEALING

Belonging to Ourselves

> *No one man can, for any considerable time, wear one*
> *face to himself, and another to the multitude, without*
> *finally getting bewildered as to which is the true one.*
>
> NATHANIEL HAWTHORNE

> *The pieces I am, she gather them and gave them*
> *back to me in all the right order.*
>
> TONI MORRISON, *BELOVED*

One day when I was in the sixth grade, I invited friends over and made the mistake of allowing them into the downstairs bedroom and letting them see what was behind a divider screen. Behind the divider screen, my mother had erected a small prayer altar, a steel tray with incense holders, and posters of Hindu deities. It was, I'm sure, unlike anything sixth grade girls in a small Alabama town had ever seen. In the hubbub, the divider fell and one of the screen glasses split and shattered. It was a frightening moment for me and for them. But what was more frightening to me was wondering what they'd think of me and my family after seeing that prayer altar. Perhaps no one would be allowed to come to my house anymore. Perhaps they would tell their parents and they'd all conclude we were part of a cult. *What strangeness is this?* they'd ask around their dinner tables, in this town with a population of around seven thousand, with the first Hindu Indian family in town. I may never know what conversations happened, but I lived with the fear of being shunned and having an invisible divider erected between me and others.

## TRAUMA AND RACIAL MELANCHOLIA

Trauma can be a single occurrence, or it can be a recurring situation and accumulate, such as if you live in a war zone or an area with more than its share of crime. Or, if you're told by your culture you don't belong and you aren't worthy enough to be here because of culture, skin color, etc., you may also experience this accumulation in varying ways on the body and psyche.

As people of color, we experience persistent cultural systemic trauma, carry the experiences of our ancestors, and experience racialized attacks directly. Trauma also results when we're not allowed to be who we are fully in our bodies solely because of skin color, when darker melanin or other physical attributes are seen as inferior or subject to ridicule. When our culture tells us we can't belong to the culture, an immediate barrier is constructed, because our identities are connected with our bodies. We are not true to ourselves, to others, or to God when we ignore or deny who we are—whether by choice or not.

When we are not fully known to ourselves, we are lonely to ourselves. In some cases we internalize the racism and develop self-hatred. When we aren't true to ourselves, others, or God, we can't have authentic intimacy. When culture rejects us, we can also reject ourselves, multiplying the trauma. We might distrust and begin to dislike ourselves. It's alienation on several levels. It's a fractured self. It's a death of the full and authentic self.

Not all of us grow up conscious of our internalized racism. I couldn't have articulated this or named it at the time I experienced it—I'm only able to name these things years later. Internalized racism occurs when minority groups or individuals absorb the racism and stereotypes from the dominant culture.[1] I knew there was something missing, and when I was in my twenties, I sought out the Indian community intentionally, to learn about the culture. I found a group of Indian people and started attending their parties and church events. The parts of myself that I had cast aside, I wanted to integrate back into myself.

I appreciate what my friend Xochitl Dixon writes: "Our differences are God's good and deliberate decisions."[2] We aren't accidents. We were created with unique abilities and personalities— and varying shades of skin. It's intentional and deliberate on God's part, not some haphazard mix-and-match slot machine with only a single ideal version of a human as the "jackpot winner."

The prolonged results of estrangement and displacement result in "racial melancholia" and "racial dissociation," terms explained by psychologists David L. Eng and Shinhee Han. They approach melancholia as a collective condition in understanding the implications of immigration, assimilation, and racialization.[3] In other words, assimilation into mainstream culture for people of color entails adopting the dominant sets of norms and ideals. Differing from these ideals or a failure to integrate them results in a state of melancholia. In fact, racial melancholia can be described as a splitting of the psyche and is observed in the concept of "colonial mimicry," which is "the ways in which a colonial regime compels the colonized subject to mimic Western ideals of whiteness.... Colonial mimicry is the desire for a reformed, recognizable Other, *as a subject of a difference that is almost the same, but not quite. . . . 'Almost the same but not white.'"*[4] The authors describe a sense of national melancholia, a "collective national haunting" because of the lack of assimilation into white mainstream culture. In fact, it is fascinating to note that "much of late-twentieth-century ethnic and immigrant literature in the U.S. is characterized by ghosts and hauntings."[5]

We've broken off parts of our identity and live as fractured pieces of our whole selves because of a lack of belonging, because of not being "allowed" to be authentic, to be completely Brown or Black. There is a compartmentalization in this fragmented existence—a dissociation of selves, a splitting of the psyche. Compartmentalization is hiding broken pieces from ourselves, explains Rich Villodas in *The Deeply Formed Life*.[6] Because certain narratives have been perpetuated in our culture, as people of color we've even forged these stereotypes about ourselves, too, creating distrust about our own selves, making "us strange to ourselves."[7]

These identity journeys and consequences have impacted generations among us today. If people are asking, "Why are we still talking about slavery or race?" it's because of those historical and present wounds, and because our systems are contributing to systemic oppression. "*There is another fragment formed of colonial power*," writes Willie James Jennings.

So many people of color understand this fragment. It is life formed in fragment, in memory of loss and in loss of memory where worlds were shattered into pieces: land and animals taken; practice and rituals, dance and songs, ancient word and inherited dream, thoughts and prayers. . . . *Many of us work in fragments*, trying to tie together, hold together, the witness of our pupils. Weaving the sounds, songs, and stories that are only fleeting echoes of what was. Call it a cultural fragment if you wish. It is serious business—precious saving work—trying to save it, unearth it, and hold it close.[8]

According to therapist Natalie Gutierrez in *The Pain We Carry*, people of color deal with a number of burdens: the cultural legacy burden, the messages our society tells us about our race and ethnicity; the family legacy burden, which include narratives and family patterns; and personal burdens, or experiences we have encountered directly, such as microaggressions or assault. Living this way can result in living in survival mode, in toxic stress, or even with posttraumatic stress disorder (PTSD).

Ethnic and racial minorities are groups in limbo, in various stages of waiting and longing, in various stages of invisibility and hypervisiblity. International students wait for visas, immigrant workers wait on court dates and visas that will allow them to keep working or stay longer to work. DACA recipients wait, and those in transitional statuses wait, constantly weighing options of where to live and how to survive. Immigrants await news from relatives on the other side of the world and live in dread of the phone ringing in the middle of the night, usually a sign of bad news. People of color wait for justice, perpetually waiting to be seen, to be known, waiting for acceptance, acknowledgment, belonging—or they fear being targeted or singled out. It is a position of ongoing exposure. To be perpetually waiting is to stand in a never-ending metaphorical queue, waiting for a "golden ticket," a "pass," a once-and-for-all-welcome, a perpetual welcome, a perpetual belonging. Perpetual waiting exacerbates the sense of racial melancholia.

## EPIGENETICS

My friend Lisa, a psychiatric nurse practitioner who used to live and work in West Africa, led a workshop a few years ago for a small group going to serve short-term in Rwanda. I wasn't going on the trip but was still welcome to attend the session. Lisa shared about an emerging field called "epigenetics," and how the trauma of the ethnic wars could manifest in the lives of the people there. The CDC defines epigenetics as "the study of how your behaviors and environment can cause changes that affect the way your genes work." But interestingly, epigenetic changes can be reversed."[9] According to Rachel Yehuda, professor of psychiatry and neuroscience:

> Research confirms that adverse experiences may influence the next generation through multiple pathways and all these channels seem to involve epigenetics: alterations in the way that genes function. Epigenetics potentially explains why effects of trauma may endure long after the immediate threat is gone, and it is also implicated in the diverse pathways by which trauma is transmitted to future generations.[10]

There can be collective trauma, as in the Rwandan genocide, or trauma on the personal level; both can be expressed in future generations. Slavery in the United States is an example of nationwide trauma that the United States is still healing from. The wounds of that era, and the implications and consequences, are with us today. This is true even if our elders or relatives are not willing to share or talk about their experiences—the experiences still live in us, and may manifest in other ways, such as unexplained anxiety or depression. But even so, our histories aren't complete without the history of our ancestors, and their journeys, their migrations, their stories of exile.

People can experience trauma not only from what they experience personally but also what they witness happening to others.[11] The coverage of the death of George Floyd is one instance in recent history that affected much of the nation, and has been cited as one of the reasons for increased interest in and sales of race-related books, influencing policies and creating awareness of racial issues.

If all this sounds like a lot, well, it is. *Allostatic load* is the cumulation of all the events, racism, discrimination, microaggression, etc. that we hold in our bodies.[12] Some other manifestations of these are holding tension in the body, hunched shoulders, clenched fists, clenched jaw and teeth (which happens to be mine), anxiety, depression, hyper-alertness, the inability to press rest/pause, sleeping issues, and other health concerns.

We also have various stress responses. Years ago, I was taught there was a fight or flight response, but now there are a couple more that are recognized: freeze or fawn.[13] Fight is the response when we choose to stay and fight, and flight means we choose to turn and run. Freeze means we pause or stall. Fawn means we attempt to appease or pacify the threat. We choose among these four responses as a response to potential trauma.

Generational trauma—the stories, the actions, and the inheritance or "gifts" that we don't want passed down but come to us anyway—are part of many of our lives. We carry the trauma and wounds so deeply in our bodies that it changes how our bodies read a DNA sequence. But if there is such a thing as generational trauma, there must also be such a thing as generational blessing. God will remain faithful and loyal for a thousand generations to those who love God (Deut 7:9). The legacies we have to pass down are much richer and bigger than only the side of pain. If trauma can change us and our brains, so can healing. As we embark on a path of healing from the traumas, generational blessings also await.

A way of bringing blessing is by breaking the cycle. It involves changing destructive behavior and communication patterns we may have had passed down in our lives. We often drift into these patterns without realizing it, as these destructive patterns feel "normal." Breaking these cycles can be difficult, but not impossible. It requires becoming self-aware and owning it. It might require therapy. But restoration of relationships brings generational blessing: restoration with self, with others, and with God—and the cycle of the harmful epigenetic pathway is broken.

One fall, I was pruning an oversized hydrangea bush whose white blooms had withered and dried. As I was cutting back the monstrosity, I discovered a fresh, white hydrangea blossom hidden underneath—the last one of the season, amid dozens of dead brown and crispy blooms. It had been sheltered and kept warm by the many stalks around and above it. I took a photo. In that moment, I wondered about the stories of hope, resilience, and flourishing—of finding the pocket of warmth, love, joy, and protection—even amid the draining and difficult. In the midst of generational trauma, there is also the hope of generational blessing.

## PTSD, RACE, DEPRESSION

About six out of every one hundred people will have PTSD at some point in their lives, and twelve million adults in the United States have PTSD during a given year.[14] This is only a small portion of those who have gone through a trauma. About 8 percent of women develop PTSD sometime in their lives compared with 4 percent of men.[15] A connection exists between race and PTSD: PTSD is more common in people of color, and racism can be a cause of PTSD. Because of this, it's recommended that mental health professionals ask clients of color about their experiences of discrimination.[16]

Every ethnic group is affected. Suicide is the leading cause of death among Asian American young adults between the ages of fifteen and twenty-four. Sixteen percent of the Black population reported having a mental illness—about seven million people.

Several studies have found that Hispanics are at greater risk for posttraumatic stress disorder than Black or non-Hispanics.[17] Indigenous populations report experiencing serious psychological stress 2.5 times more than the general population over a month's time and are more likely to abuse alcohol and drugs at earlier ages and at higher rates than all ethnic groups. Access to health care is limited due to the isolated and rural locations of many Indigenous communities. Twice as many Indigenous people live in poverty compared to the rest of the US population,[18] and they experience historical trauma,[19] manifesting in ways such as a breakdown of traditional Native family values, substance abuse, depression, PTSD, and domestic violence.[20]

An Afghan teenager (who fled after the Taliban took over Afghanistan) I happened to meet had shaved her head out of anger and emotion. She was processing the trauma of her experience. When we see these folks in our neighborhood, hear of them in a sound bite on the radio, or read a line or two in a news article, we aren't usually aware of the depth of trauma they may be experiencing. These Afghan women, fortunate to leave, live with the guilt of being free and safe and leaving those left behind: their family members, their sisters, their aunts, grandmas, cousins, their friends. Women are banned from receiving an education in Afghanistan with very little freedom, the only country in the world with such a ban.[21] Those who couldn't leave are now living as shadows in an oppressive state.

## IN-BETWEEN TIME

We live in "in-between" time—in between life and death, on earth, in a place veiled from heaven, but not entirely removed from it. Madeleine L'Engle, one of my favorite authors, writes about a tesseract as a way of traveling through time and space in *A Wrinkle in*

*Time*. In her book *Walking on Water*, she talks about *chronos* time and *kairos* time. *Chronos* time is clock time, measurable in terms of minutes and seconds and days. It is chronological time.

*Kairos* time is qualitative, not quantitative, time. It measures moments, not seconds. It can be considered a moment of ripeness, such as in Ecclesiastes 3:1: "There is a time for everything, and a season for every activity under the heavens." The ancient Indians also had an equivalent for *kairos* called *ritu*. It's a Sanskrit word with a sense of spirituality connected to it, acknowledging that something will happen at "the right time." Ritu is used today by Hindus for the timing of certain rituals and ceremonies. L'Engle describes *kairos* time as "real time. God's time. That time which breaks through chronos with a shock of joy, that time we do not recognize while we are experiencing it, but only afterwards, because kairos has nothing to do with chronological time."[22] In the Christian faith tradition, we live in the "in-between" stage of a kingdom not yet come in full.

Living in this in-between time as in-between people can be disorienting. I don't particularly like the uncertainty, and I'm worried about being left alone, wandering in the desert and wilderness of perplexing times. I want to know there is comfort at the end of each day, that God has not abandoned me. I want to know that where I am, I'll feel that I belong there—and not like a wanderer who has lost her way home, for an unknown length of time. I long for certainty, assurance, care, belonging. Who chooses exile and wandering or the in-between? Yet much of life is lived in this space of in-between, in seasons of waiting. Exile drops us in uncertainty, unknowing, disbelonging. Yet maybe that is the start of our journey home and a place of greater hope. Maybe exile *is* the journey to belonging. Maybe ethnic loneliness and disbelonging are mountains we must pass on the journey to belonging.

We live in multidimensional time; it isn't all in a linear direction. The concept of *kairos* helps me to understand that there is a better thing happening beyond, in "tesseracts," in regions beyond space and time, that beautiful things are afoot, which are not yet visible or present in chronos time. The burdens of the past, the memories, the pains, the trauma, the legacies as well as the bountiful, good, and beautiful are working out into a story I cannot yet realize. The waiting has purpose. Time is a ripening fruit. But even so, amid the waiting, on the road to belonging, I must learn how to live with boundaries so I do not allow myself to stumble into deep valleys or off of steep cliffs.

## BOUNDARIES

There is a saying in Hindi, *Log kya kahenge?* which means "What will people say?" This is a common question and concern. We wonder what everyone will think. *Will they approve? Judge us? Support us? Criticize us? Cut us off?* There may be peer or community pressure to behave or do things a certain way in certain communities of color. Thus, learning how to establish healthy boundaries as we walk these in-between roads, on our way to a better place, becomes a task some of us have had to learn the hard way. But having healthy boundaries is a necessity for all of us.

Healthy boundaries suggest we have carved out intentional space for our spiritual, physical, emotional, and social lives. In the survey I conducted, an East African respondent shared that to feel a sense of belonging, she needs "curiosity, compassion, respect, humor, love, kindness, thoughtfulness, space, and boundaries." Our boundaries help us belong to ourselves and guard us from toxic and unsafe people. A healthy boundary means we have exercised time-management skills to make sure we are getting enough rest, exercising, staying well hydrated, eating nutritious foods, and allowing time for play and fun. Our boundaries assist us in prioritizing the need for spiritual rest and for solitude. They enable us to allow time for friendship and meaningful relationships.

But what if some others repeatedly cross the boundaries? Then maybe it's time to reassess the relationship. But what if it's society and its structures that continue to deny or gaslight us? How can we respond if society keeps telling us what we're experiencing is not real and not acknowledging our experience as a person of color? We can't just walk away from society and live as a hermit. A counselor or therapist can be a helpful guide in setting good boundaries around our time and energy, but here are a few ways to get started yourself.[23]

- Build a small circle of confidants. This could be just a few people you can trust, who are a safe place for you to vent, decompress, cry, laugh, complain, talk with; people who won't judge you but stand with you through your experience, people who offer love and authentic connection. Find safe places where you're known, you are seen, and you don't have to explain yourself. Ideally, this group of people also understands the cultural differences you live with.

  - Stay accountable to a friend. Find someone you trust and check in with each other regularly. Share your frustrations and anger rather than letting them fester and turn to bitterness.

  - Find a small group or church group to share life together. The point is not just to meet for the sake of meeting but to find a group where you can stick together long-term, as you seek to be part of a larger faith community. If you're working through church hurt, find a support group or seek help in working through that experience.

  - Go to those who love you.

- Establish healthy boundaries.

  - Learn how to say no. In some of our ethnic communities, we have strong values of not wanting to disappoint our elders. But learning how to say no promotes self-care and rest, and prevents burnout. It's okay to say no. I've had to tell myself this over and over: *you can say no.*

  - You may feel burned out by being the "token person of color," the one who is always called on to educate others or asked questions about race, on top of the exhaustion you already experience defending your place and existence. There may be times when walking away will be the right decision. There may be times when you will decide to stay. Both are potential and valid options.

  - Figure out what you're going to say yes to. Kirsten Powers, in *Saving Grace,* says yes to "respectful dialogue and debate, constructive criticism, honesty, good-faith debates, humility, kindness, and support for justice and equality."[24] That's her list, but you can create your own.

  - If you are in a space where you are not respected or feeling unsafe, consider how to leave or how to create margin for yourself if it is impossible to leave. Talk to someone you trust about plausible options.

  - Limit your news. We don't (and shouldn't) live under rocks, but news can be distressing and increases your exposure to vicarious trauma. Limit your time and choose your sources.

  - Limit social media. Keep it in short, intentional doses. It sets up the comparison game as we view the curated images others share. We get sucked into others' drama. Turn off notifications. Stop doom scrolling. Spend time with actual people, not social media outrage.

- Dream. Write down what you dream and envision or create a vision board. Don't allow cynicism to harden your heart against all that is good and beautiful, against all the love and acceptance you do experience.

- Operate from a place of hope. Continue to remind yourself of this: *you have not yet met all the people who will love you.* That sentence has encouraged me time and time again.

- Pay attention to your internal dialogue. J. S. Park in his book *The Voices We Carry* talks about the voice he heard in his head regarding belonging that said, "You are not one of us."[25] Name those voices that want to dehumanize or degrade you. Write them down in one column. Then write down the opposite of that statement in the next column. Speak that positive list over yourself. Pray over that list. Believe it to be true.

- Intentionally build rest into your life. Find restorative practices that are calming and healing, such as prayer, yoga, walking, or a hobby you enjoy. Light a candle, schedule time for listening to music, read, spend time in nature, or select another activity that restores you. Pay attention to your body. Don't ignore the signs of stress and the need for rest.

- Practice self-care. What works for you? Journaling, praying, carving out time to read a book, painting, talking with a friend, walking in the woods, exercising, napping? Find that and add it intentionally to your routine.

- Stay tender. See the world with wonder. Be curious. Be on guard for indifference. One of the best ways to stay tender and hopeful is by keeping a gratitude list. Every day, write down three things you are thankful for.

- Stay curious and hopeful. Frederick Buechner said, "Here is the world. Beautiful and terrible things will happen. Don't be afraid."[26] We know that there will be hard things to contend with during life, but there are, and will also be, beautiful things.

- Read the Psalms. In the Psalms, David and other psalmists cry out to God with songs of lament, grief, sorrow, joy, and praise. They question God, ask about evildoers, share their doubts, shake their fists at God; they share trust in God for deliverance, for companionship, for hope. It's an honest wellspring of the gamut of human experience. Don't be afraid to voice all your questions, frustrations, doubts, and concerns to God.

- Keep a sense of humor. Don't take everything so seriously. Laugh at yourself. Laughter is medicine—and it's free. No need to wait and see how much insurance will pay for this kind of medicine! Find something to laugh about regularly.

- Deal with anger. One of the challenging questions is what to do with the anger we feel.

  - First, name it. Acknowledge the anger. But it's vital to not let the harms destroy you. Don't allow your life to be ruled by fear and your existence to be swallowed up by anger.

  - Channel that anger by serving others in your community or doing something for someone else that aligns with your gifts and callings. It doesn't have to be activist work—anything to serve someone else qualifies. It takes the focus off ourselves and enlarges our perspective.

- Consider finding a mentor. Learn from those who are a few steps ahead of you and can support you. Having a mentor can help you process experiences with someone who is more objective and removed from the situation than you. It can also help in dealing with bitterness and anger and bouncing off ideas before responding. Choose wisely.

- Knowing and learning your racial identity, understanding internalized racism, grieving and naming it, and reclaiming your whole self are a few steps in the process of healing.[27] Go back through some of the questions at the end of each chapter in this book and journal your thoughts, and read books such as *Beyond Colorblind*, *Healing Racial Trauma*, *Mixed Blessing*, and *The Minority Experience*.

- Practice joy. A stunning poem by J. Drew Lanham, an African American naturalist, ornithologist, and writer, starts off with these words: "Joy is the justice we give ourselves."[28] Joy is justice you give yourself. Joy is resistance. Joy is activism. Joy is for you. (The entire poem is worth reading.)

These steps won't solve everything, but they are practical ways to help you feel less alone. What you're going through matters. Don't believe the lie that you are alone. There are many who are experiencing this also and want to walk alongside you.

This list isn't exhaustive. Don't try to incorporate everything at once. I have to remind myself that I can't expect myself to know all the answers or to balance this tension perfectly. I will continue to make mistakes. I give myself permission to be human. I remind myself that I am regularly entering new territory as a person of color. Each time I walk into a new room, a new office, a new gathering, a new event, or I meet a new person, it's like walking in a new country or a new city. It's new territory, and I'm learning the skills necessary to walk on that terrain and to give grace to myself. Establishing emotional safety is a gift I give myself.

• • •

In the book of Job, we read that Job dealt with severe loss and trauma. Job was a righteous and prosperous man who faced a series of devastating trials, losing everything: his family, his property and wealth, as well as his health. He experiences profound suffering and emotional and physical anguish. As he tries to make sense of his predicament, some friends visit him and offer explanations, but the attempts are not helpful. As Job continues to wrestle with his suffering and notions of God's justice, he laments, grieves, mourns, and expresses his pain and frustration. Through it all, despite the suffering, he refuses to curse God, and he maintains his faith. God responds to Job's questions and concerns, emphasizing the omniscience and omnipotence of God, and the limited knowledge of human understanding. Job humbles himself before God, and in the end, God restores Job's fortunes, blessing him more abundantly than before. Job's story is encouragement for us. In the midst of severe trauma and loss, it is possible to find renewed hope and healing, and experience the restoration of years that were lost, "years the locusts have eaten" (Joel 2:25).

I do recognize that complete liberation and full healing cannot happen until there is recognition and healing and change in our society. Yet, our flourishing necessitates that we name and acknowledge the trauma, and live holistically and in ways true to ourselves. We learn from the past and hold the truths we learn while we live in the present and look toward the future; we live in both *chronos* and *kairos* time. What we can control is our response and our own decision to choose to heal. That means establishing healthy boundaries and practicing self-care.

Belonging to ourselves means knowing ourselves and taking care of ourselves. Our exiled states, our loneliness, our liminal spaces of belonging, are the very places where we discover true belonging and authentic kinship with our exiled self. Your joy is a gift to yourself. Your safety and boundaries are gifts you give yourself—and your full and complete self is not only a gift you bring to the world, but it also honors the God who fashioned you in a very particular way.

## SO, WHAT ARE YOU?

You are the product of the past
But you are also the present
And the future
You are full of potential and promise
Your inner dialogue speaks of hope
And gratitude
You are here, you are welcome
You are calm, you are grounded
You have drawn a safe line
Around yourself
You are not what was done to you
You are not what was said to you
You are a flourishing child of glory
And wild wonder
You know who you are
Your safety, your space, your joy—
Are gifts you give yourself
And others, and the world
And God

## QUESTIONS FOR REFLECTION
## AND DISCUSSION

1. What specific measures from the bullet point list in this chapter do you feel you need to put in place to protect your health and well-being right now? Pick no more than two or three to focus on at a time in the coming months.

2. Healing starts with acknowledgment. Name your pains, heartaches, disappointments, sorrows, and abuses. Acknowledge what was lost, either to you, or your family, or your ancestors.

3. What traumas do you need healing from in your life? Which ones have been passed on to you? Spend time writing, praying, reflecting. Pray over them and ask God for wisdom and guidance in taking steps toward healing.

4. Writing prompts:

- "I can take care of myself by . . ."
- "I will no longer try to fix . . ."
- "I learned to listen to myself when . . ."

# 8

# SHARING OUR STORIES

## BELONGING TO OTHERS

*It has been said that next to hunger and thirst, our*
*most basic human need is for storytelling.*

KHALIL GIBRAN

*Being listened to is so close to being loved that*
*most people don't know the difference.*

DAVID AUGSBURGER

Over twenty years ago, *Interpreter of Maladies*, a book of short stories by Jhumpa Lahiri, won the Pulitzer Prize. When I heard the name of the author and the subject matter—the immigrant life of South Asian Indians—I obtained a copy and began reading.

I was stunned by this book. For the first time, I was reading stories by someone who looked like me about people who looked like me, living life in the West, who weren't caricatures or stereotypes, who were humanized South Asians. I saw myself in the stories by Lahiri. Her observations were keen and accurate. She wrote with nuance of the reality of being an immigrant and captured details that other South Asian immigrants would understand.

I proceeded to read every book she wrote and remain a huge fan of her work.

At the time, I was writing but only for myself. Writing was a part of my identity I hadn't yet named publicly, but Lahiri's work gave me the imagination to move beyond my limited belief in myself. To this day, I give her credit for opening my eyes to what the writing of a diasporic South Asian could be. She opened my heart and mind to the possibility I could also be a writer.

## OUR GENERATIONAL STORIES

During the brutal and arduous journey when my mother's grandparents and her aunt Prem fled Pakistan for India during the Partition of 1947, my mother's aunt became ill with pneumonia, and she never recovered. After my great-grandparents and great-aunt Prem made it safely to India, which wasn't a given as thousands did not survive, my great-grandfather tried to find treatments, visiting doctor after doctor. My mother, the eldest of six, remembers spending one summer in the Himalayan foothills while her parents and grandparents sought local healers who used herbs and other natural treatments after finding no other medicines that worked. My great-aunt survived the Partition, but she eventually died in her thirties, and no one is quite sure of the diagnosis.

Aunt Prem lives on in the memories of those who experienced that event. These stories leave an indelible mark on us—and though I was born two generations later, they are also part of my story. The trauma of the past is carried on—we don't experience it in the same way as those who experienced it firsthand, but we carry something of it in varying degrees. Aunt Prem's story is part of our family history, and we'll continue to tell the story so we do not forget.

## OUR HISTORIES AND STORIES

In most cases we didn't learn our ethnic histories while we were in school—especially if we were raised in the United States. I remember sitting in my Western Civilization class in college, a required course, wondering what was happening around the rest of the world while I was memorizing the reigns of British monarchs. What happens when we learn the histories of one another? It erodes suspicion between us. It's heartening to see more colleges adding Black history, Asian history, and Indigenous history courses as options of study, but we've got a long way to go. Books such as *The Making of Asian America* and *The Warmth of Other Suns* are good places to start.

"We pursue beauty in difference, not in reflections of ourselves," writes Shannan Martin in *Start with Hello*.[1] Being curious about others is a way to expand our perspectives. As we seek to learn about others, we can move to the next step of creating welcoming spaces. Being curious and fostering our imaginations to develop a society that prioritizes belonging are ways we love our neighbor and curb the feeling of aloneness.

Knowing our histories, understanding them, and sharing them is essential. Let's initiate a transformation by learning our histories—our personal, family, and cultural stories. Learn and own your ethnic story, and read others' stories. If we fear what we don't know, then we can't love what we don't know—and "there is no fear in love. But perfect love drives out fear" (1 Jn 4:18). Reading other BIPOC stories helps me to, as Adrian Pei writes, "recognize that I am walking down a path of emotional realities that countless others have walked before me—and which countless others will walk in the future."[2] Our stories reflect a God who loves diversity.

Last fall I attended an event where I heard the stories of Latina, Korean, and African women sharing words of identity and belonging. Listening to these stories read aloud was even more compelling than reading them on paper alone. Listening to ethnic minority stories has not only helped me to heal but has also helped in my identity formation. Indeed, as Martin writes, our collective humanity is at stake when we are stuck in our own echo chambers and neglect to listen to the wide diversity of stories around us.[3]

Books and stories are essential, but the reality is that even a life-changing, beautiful book isn't the same as an embodied human standing in front of me, telling her story with the nuance of tone, gesture, and feeling. I not only need the written word but also the spoken word. I need to see and hear the stories of belonging and disbelonging in person.

Listening and sharing aren't easy, even when we are trying to help one another. It's vulnerable. It takes courage to share and show up, and it requires time and intentionality. But it's vital. In a world of abundant noise, busyness, and isolation, there is a lack of embodied listening. Our society in the West favors "talkers." It feels countercultural to make a concerted commitment to listen to others, especially to stories of those different from us. But "earth's crammed with heaven"[4] and that means the earth is not only full of natural wonders but also full of beautiful stories, and we honor one another by telling, sharing, and listening to our stories of disbelonging, loneliness, searching, and joy.

## SHARING IN SAFE SPACES

For those of you who have found it difficult to find a group with a similar background, I can empathize. I didn't have anyone to talk to about growing up as an Indian Desi (people from the Indian subcontinent who live in other countries) for years. But it doesn't have to be this way today. With more diversity (thanks to immigration) in our cities and with the benefits of technology (and a good use of it), it's easier to find your people.

You could join (or start) a Be the Bridge group or similar group. Or create a support group of people of color and check in with one another monthly. I would suggest being careful not to make it a gripe session. Make sure you speak of that which is hopeful too. Also, share with the idea that this is a safe space and establish some initial ground rules to make it a safe space.

Another suggestion when sharing our stories is what Latasha Morrison recommends for white people as they learn about racism, and it can be a guideline for people of color to remember too:[5]

Don't deflect racism
Don't defend racism
Don't deny racism

Affirm one another as you share your stories. Affirm your experiences, acknowledge the pain. Share your heart and then pray over it. Your story could be your family history, situations you've encountered, how you're dealing with microaggressions, or how God is redeeming your ethnic identity. Any of these qualify. The purpose isn't to have a plan of action (though you can if you decide you need to). The purpose is to construct a support group for each other. Take advantage of the fact that you know people who are like you, people of color going through day-to-day life like you. And if you don't know people in your community, get involved in your local community and church, volunteer for a cause you care about. If you cannot get involved that way, perhaps you can find an online group. If it turns out you no longer need a support group, that is fine; there are times and seasons. But we all need community and friendship always, in every season, and someone to listen and help us process any "othering" we experience.

The danger of this kind of support is getting stuck in and never leaving an ethnic enclave. Instead use this space as a safe space of belonging for you. It isn't meant to be the only place you live. Venture beyond and befriend all kinds of people (always keeping in mind healthy boundaries). I recognize for some of our elders, enclaves were the only viable option, or they were what was most comfortable. We respect them and their situation, and we discern it could be different for us.

## SPEAKING UP

In 2016, Chanté, a Black journalist, decided to go natural. As soon as she stopped straightening her hair, and cut it short, however, people began to treat her differently. In 2019 she read a newspaper article about Black students who were being kicked out of school for wearing their natural hair. Upset by the discrimination she and these students were experiencing, she decided to use her journalism to educate the public about the issue, including covering California's passage of the CROWN Act, which stands for "Create a Respectful and Open World for Natural Hair." As more than twenty states have passed similar legislation, Chanté has continued writing about this issue, using her words to advocate for racial justice.[6]

As people of color, we've had to adjust ourselves to the prevailing norms and cultural preferences around us. When is it safe to speak up in the workplace if all of one's colleagues or superiors are white? When is it safe to speak up in a social setting among all white peers? When is it safe to speak up in a community group or church among mostly white members? A person of color dances and balances around various lines all the while learning what the lines are, when they shift, and when and if they should be crossed. Work norms are different from social ones: knowing when to speak, how to speak, and even how to wear one's hair are standards we are continually navigating and learning. There is a cost to speaking out and speaking up. We weigh the costs/benefits and pros/cons in our minds. Author and speaker Kathy Khang writes that, specifically for women of color, we sit in the intersection of race and gender. Speaking up labels us as threatening or countercultural, and even when we are silent, we are still communicating something.[7]

We can find confidence within ourselves, the truth and conviction that our voice is essential and it matters, but the other piece—that others will applaud when we show up and walk into a room as who we are—we can't control. In fact, we must be prepared for denial, hostility, rejection, aggression, and silencing. Ultimately, we can't control how others respond, but we can control what *we* do.

As we work out the ways we belong to others, we eventually will discern if and what kind of involvement we will have in justice work. Not everyone is an activist, or a protester carrying signs or chanting in the street. There are many other ways to speak up and get involved, which do not require being front and center. As we do our own identity formation work, we may find ourselves unable to participate in anything but our own survival or healing, and that is completely okay. There may (or may not) be seasons when we feel a nudge to "do something." In *Social Justice for the Sensitive Soul*, author Dorcas Cheng-Tozun walks us through the gifts of all kinds of change-makers, and especially how we can participate in quieter ways that are for sensitive souls.

## DON'T COLLUDE WITH INVISIBILITY

One day I asked my counselor why I felt invisible in certain situations. In some cases, I knew I was deliberately being left out. But in other instances, I couldn't figure out why I felt that way. Then she asked me a surprising question: In what ways was I "colluding with invisibility"? It made me pause. She told me an interpretation of the story and Mary and Martha, one I hadn't heard, to explain.

We tend to hear the story about Mary and Martha in a certain way: Martha is the busybody, the doer, the one who can't sit still and is anxious about getting everything done. Somebody has to get the work done, right? We're taught that Mary is the one who is eagerly sitting at Jesus' feet, soaking up his wisdom. Maybe Mary is shirking responsibility, but she's often portrayed as the type B personality—calm, cool, and collected. Either way, Jesus says she has chosen the better thing. Is Mary the example here and Martha isn't? But perhaps Martha is hiding. Maybe she knows some truth will be exposed—and her heart will be cracked open—and she is reluctant. Maybe she's avoiding vulnerability and conviction.

What does this mean? The point of the story isn't only about the personalities of Mary and Martha (although that could be one aspect and many interpretations of this story are valid). Maybe the point of the story is that Jesus is once again upsetting the status quo with a woman sitting at Jesus' feet. This is not the usual way of doing things. This is not how women were treated in that time period and cultural context. The invitation he offers is for Martha to join in too. The space is there for both of them to be near—just as men were. The lesson is one of access and inclusion.

It was a radical move for the day. And it's a different interpretation of this passage than what I'd considered. The question I was being asked is, Was I also hiding from the truth of who I was invited to be? Was I also colluding with invisibility? How was I shrinking back, not speaking up, and putting aside pieces of myself?

And here was my invitation: I didn't have to choose to be invisible. I could choose to bring all of me to the table, to the story of my own life. I could invite myself to the table—and invite others as well. I realized I had long been walking around looking for validation that I didn't belong. It was confirmation to me that I needed to pay attention. We have confirmation we belong, so we walk with moral courage and cautious optimism but also with a double dose of reality.

As an Asian American and as a BIPOC woman, I often feel invisible, so this idea felt strange. This collusion with invisibility isn't about victim blaming (myself) but about bringing all of myself to the table. That isn't to say that all of a sudden bringing my whole self will automatically result in acceptance. It won't. It doesn't mean that I should bring all the pieces of myself and lay them out on the table always. That's not wise or advisable. I can't control wider aspects of society and what happens when I walk into a room. But I can control my own sense of belonging and carry it within myself, as my healing and boundaries allow. It does mean I am true to myself and true to who God made me to be. That is the part I have control over.

I can't control the culture at-large. I can speak up, speak out, write, pray, think, share my story, and work for small or big changes at a time, but I still have little or no control over what my efforts (or anyone's efforts) may produce. Culture change is long. Attitude changes are long. Acceptance is long. This is a long game, a long haul. It is something we may or may not see the fruit of in our lifetimes. But I do have control over living my full, authentic life to the degree I can. Rosa Parks did that. Harriet Tubman did that. Martin Luther King Jr. did that. And here's the remarkable thing: so did thousands and thousands of others who don't have their names written in history books. Everyday people like us are showing us the way to belonging—and it's often in quiet, subtle ways that don't involve TV cameras or viral social media posts.

I know I can't expect belonging in all spaces, but I have to pay attention to the places where I do belong. Should I expect belonging?

Here's where I have to check myself. *Who is defining belonging for me?* In God's definition, I *do* belong. *Do I believe this?* Will I live my life believing this truth about myself? I also have to check myself to remain open and guard against becoming hardhearted. How can I remain softhearted and still be safe?

I think the key is knowing to whom I belong. First is finding the belonging to myself. "Love your neighbor as yourself" (Mt 22:39). Loving ourselves is that first step. Then, we can love others well and from a place of safety and softness. I can love others while still maintaining my healthy boundaries. I can find relationships where there is a mutual and healthy give-and-take. I can find places where there is genuine authenticity.

I can go slow, realizing that authentic relationship will produce fruit in time. With the assurance of belonging with safe people and my safe community, I can venture out when I feel called or led and safe to do so. I have the backing, the foundation, and the belonging I need from other sources. Our strength isn't from our own selves, our own personal resources, but what we can do together, and who we are together. We aren't meant to be solitary trees. "Our neural, hormonal, and genetic makeup support interdependence over independence."[8] We aren't living just for ourselves, and we weren't designed to.

Perhaps part of the problem is we don't know how to belong anymore. What does it look like to reconnect in our digital, social media, post-pandemic world, where we're seeing high degrees of social anxiety and people feeling safer in physical isolation? We have to learn how to belong to one another all over again. And that doesn't happen when we're always by ourselves or communicating predominantly through digital and social media. We cannot survive by the dopamine hits on our brains through likes and comments and pretend it's the same as an authentic relationship. I acknowledge that there are positive and helpful connections occurring online for many of us. But it's not the same and not a substitute.

With the advent of AI technologies, which mimic words and images that look real but are fake, we are going to hunger even more for the authentic and embodied presence of one another. There is such nuance and genuine depth in an embodied relationship that a digital device cannot duplicate, and chemical communications during the give-and-take of in-person conversation that cannot be delivered over fiber optics.

Being around others is undoubtedly risky. We don't want to get hurt. We want to protect ourselves. But finding a place where we feel safe doesn't mean isolating ourselves. In isolation, we can't process our lives or grow in healthy ways socially, emotionally, or spiritually. It might be helpful to think of it this way: we have a safe small group or a few friends where we can truly be ourselves. We recognize that this core group has our best interest in mind and will support us. Our group is a soft space to land as we go beyond that circle of kindreds.

Last year, I joined a group of Asian Americans who were meeting a couple of times monthly to discuss ideas and questions, talk about faith and deconstruction, and read and discuss books together. There were specific ground rules established for our time together, such as confidentiality and listening with respect. Having these specific rules shared at the outset made a difference to me personally in my level of safety in sharing. It was a space where I didn't have to explain my Asianness and the in-betweenness, a place where others knew and understood what I was going through, even though our specific experiences would be different and we came from different countries in Asia. Though I have kind and empathetic white friends, they cannot automatically understand what it means to live in my Brown skin or as an ethnic minority.

There is a basic level of knowing, of understanding, that I do not have to explain that other Asian Americans understand.

How can we live in close relationship? Proximity is a first step, because "it is not easy to hate people close up."[9] A first step is not a solution, however; it is a *first step*. Certainly, we can't do anything if we're miles apart. It works both ways, for both sides of a relationship, for people of color, for white people. It's much harder to hate someone when we're near them and both seeking genuine community. How can we start? We can start with the dinner table, a coffee date, a walk around the block.

We know, however, that proximity is not enough—we know we must address larger systemic issues. That requires a different kind of work, such as through policy change and advocacy work. Both are necessary.

It's okay to allow for some discomfort in our conversations. We won't agree on everything. It's okay to allow awkward silences. It doesn't mean something is wrong. That's where we lean in, instead of draw back. It's a natural part of conversation. A little discomfort isn't bad. We step closer and accept the challenge of community, with all of its awkwardness and uncertainties. We stumble through the clumsy parts together.

One day I happened across a video online of a neuron with its dendrites lengthening. There are eighty-six billion neurons in the human brain, and each neuron is connected to one thousand other neurons, forming a complex communication system. Our neurons are looking for other neurons. Their job is to receive and communicate signals. They require a network of other neurons to function and do their job. Our bodies are designed at the cellular level to communicate in complex communication networks. We lean in close to each other because, just like at the cellular level, we are seeking those connections.

## SHARING OUR STORIES: WHY IT MATTERS

In *The Ungrateful Refugee*, Dina Nayeri shares the story of her family's escape from Iran, and the state of perpetual waiting as a refugee: homeless, stateless, no control over her home, food, or health. She explains the term *asylum-seeker* as too mild. As refugees, they were "ravenous" to belong somewhere, to not be in a perpetual state of homelessness. "How do you survive the memory of so much waiting?" she asks.[10] This kind of interminable, perpetual waiting is a situation I can only attempt to understand and learn about through reading stories.

Sharing our stories and our experience of ethnic loneliness is a vital step toward creating a more inclusive, empathetic, and understanding environment. Sharing increases awareness. We grow in empathy and understanding because we have a deeper understanding of the causes and consequences of ethnic loneliness. The more diverse stories we share and hear, the more we experience the benefits of crosscultural relationships and challenge stereotypes and biases. Sharing stories leads to the sharing of dialogue and the creation of supportive environments. The more we talk openly in society about ethnic loneliness, the more likely others are to take action to combat ethnic loneliness. Raising awareness about ethnic loneliness and sharing our stories and experiences create the opportunity to make lasting change by shaping attitudes and behaviors over time, which leads to a more empathetic and supportive society.

As BIPOC, we can continue putting our stories out there in the white-majority culture too. We need multiple and multidimensional narratives, over and over and consistently, because as we've learned, most stories in mainstream media do not represent diverse viewpoints or experiences. In fact, children's books are eight times more likely to feature an animal than a person of color.[11] Dear

BIPOC family, we need your stories (and we need publishers to publish them).

## TELL YOUR STORY

King David once saw a beautiful woman from his balcony and instantly was smitten. Bathsheba was married to someone else, but David decided it wasn't an obstacle; he was the king, after all, and could have anything he wanted. He concocted a scenario to remove this man from the picture and steal his wife. Though it's clear to us reading the story what he had done, David could not see his own selfishness.

Nathan, a prophet, approached David and told him the poignant story of two men. One man was rich and had many animals and sheep. The other man was very poor and owned only one lamb. But he loved this lamb very much, raised it with his children, shared food with the lamb, and let the lamb sleep in his arms. One day a traveler came through the town to the rich man's house, but the rich man refused to slaughter one of his sheep or cattle as a meal for the traveler, so he stole the lamb from the poor man. Upon hearing this story, David was enraged at the idea of someone stealing the poor man's one precious lamb, and declared the wealthy man should pay for what he had done. And then Nathan said to him, "You are the man!" Then it dawned on David he had behaved in a similar way by stealing someone else's wife (2 Sam 11–12).

A story woke David up. It wasn't a reprimand by a friend, a cute quote placed strategically on a mantel, or a social media post, but a story that pierced his heart. King David was surrounded by guards and a household of people. Did anyone else rebuke him, question his actions, or speak up? Maybe others dared not speak up at the risk of getting kicked out or worse. We aren't told, but it's likely David wouldn't have understood, because it took a story to open his eyes.

"Stories make us more alive, more human, more courageous, more loving," writes Madeleine L'Engle.[12] Curiosity, wonder, and imagination are becoming lost in our impulsive, impatient, consumerist culture. As we proceed through our days at breakneck speed, one of the ways we can return to a place of belonging and understanding, to connectedness, is through story.

Reading Sarah Shin's book *Beyond Colorblind* and the stories of other people of color finding their identity was a turning point for me. I needed to read those stories. It was hard reading. I had to put the book down halfway and contend with the memories and emotions the book was stirring up inside. But upon finishing the stories, I was a changed person. I had been healed in a way I needed to be healed—in naming and claiming my own ethnic identity. As I have been digesting stories of immigrants, memoirs, and books written by people of color, they have strengthened and fed me in a way nothing else could. Each story is unique, and I learn something valuable from another's experience. They remind me I'm not alone. I feel my place of belonging in humanity in a new way through the medium of story. If you're feeling lonely, reading stories can help.

It's helped me understand others. I can't fully understand what it means to be Chinese American, Korean American, or African American, so I read stories by Cathy Park Hong, Min Jin Lee, Amy Tan, Viola Davis, Andre Henry, Natasha Sistrunk Robinson, Austin Channing Brown, Ta-Nehisi Coates, and Jesmyn Ward. I can't fathom what it must feel like to be a refugee, so I read stories by Daniel Nayeri and Dina Nayeri. I can't understand the story of getting lost and then getting adopted, so I read *A Long Way Home* by Saroo Brierley. I don't know what it's like to escape the oppression of Central America and flee to America with "coyotes," so I read a story called *Solito*. In *Here We Are: American Dreams, American Nightmares* by Aarti Shahani, I read a version of an Indian immigrant family's story that was unlike most others' experiences. I read the story of Wajahat Ali, an Indian Muslim and his family. I read the stories of refugees from Sudan, *They Poured Fire on Us from the Sky*, and a story of a refugee from North Korea, *The Girl With Seven Names*. Those stories helped me understand what it's like to walk in another's shoes.

Reading about similarities found within stories that are different from my experiences tells me I also belong here, and I grow in my empathy for others. Stories help me to see my place in humanity. It's helped me immensely by not simply reading stories by people who look like me or who are in the majority culture, or have the same viewpoints in regard to ideology, religion, or politics, but by digesting a wide variety of viewpoints. The stories I have read have been utterly stunning, beautiful, tragic, and eye-opening—I can't go back now to reading the same thing. The same books. The same authors. I've tasted the stories of multiple voices and viewpoints, and while I do not always agree, I've been significantly challenged to listen, to seek, to understand, and to love those whose viewpoints and experiences are vastly different from my own. I need the stories of my own people, definitely, but I had been stuck in an echo chamber *for so long*. The authors of *Inalienable* name this danger, especially for the American Christian:

> We've been complicit in fostering such attitudes within our own echo chambers, where most of the people speaking into our lives look and think like us and only reinforce our existing beliefs. . . . Nevertheless, many American Christians still struggle to see Christians from other parts of the world as equals—especially from the developing countries in Africa, Latin America, and Asia often referred to as the global South.[13]

If Christians can't see other Christians from other nations as equals, then how are they seeing non-Christians? Everyone else? We belong at a table with people from every tribe and tongue, every nation, and each one has a place. Each one has a story to share. All our voices belong.

In the second chapter of the book of Acts, the disciples were gathered around the temple for Pentecost, a Jewish festival occurring fifty days after Passover. And on this day, the Holy Spirit fell upon all those present, and the disciples began to speak in different languages other than their own. Interestingly, those listening were able to hear the words presented to them in their very own language. It was a miracle not only in speaking but also in *hearing*.

When we share our stories, we can be assured that God will take care of making sure the stories are heard where they need to be heard. God will address the *hearing*. We just have to do the sharing—the rest isn't really up to us. "So neither the one who plants nor the one who waters is anything, but only God, who makes things grow" (1 Cor 3:7).

We are keepers of multiple legacies, and our places of othering do not have to be places of isolation, but rather places where we can invite others to walk with us and share our stories. Tell your stories to yourself. Tell your stories to each other. Tell your stories, cries, joys, laments, and songs. We recognize our shared humanity through sharing our stories. We are each a story, with unique lines, verses, rhyme, rhythm, and alliteration, with different plots, scenes, and different endings and beginnings. Put your story out in the world. Someone needs to hear it. And you will be healed and blessed by sharing it.

## SO, WHAT ARE YOU?

You are a work of art

A poem, a landscape of beauty

A story of joy, wonder, love
Your culture, your identity,
Your ethnicity
Are all created by a God
Who crafted and chiseled
The many parts of you
Into a captivating, delightful
Masterpiece
A story
With the perfect beginning
Middle, and ending
Our stories are gifts
We give to one another
Our stories are lights
Pointing to a multiethnic land
Where every tribe and tongue
Stands side by side

## QUESTIONS FOR REFLECTION
## AND DISCUSSION

1. What stories have been passed down to you from your family that are particularly meaningful for you? What stories do you want to leave behind for the generations to come?

2. In what ways have you been walking in the world seeking invisibility or "looking for confirmation you don't belong"?[14]

3. Writing prompts:
   - "The story I want to tell is . . ."
   - "I love my story because . . ."

# 9

# FROM DISBELONGING TO BELONGING

*We are each other's harvest; we are each other's business;*
*we are each other's magnitude and bond.*

GWENDOLYN BROOKS

*If we have no peace, it is because we have*
*forgotten that we belong to each other.*

MOTHER TERESA

A few years ago, I had the opportunity to fulfill a lifelong dream to visit California and see the magnificent redwood trees. Redwood trees are the tallest trees on earth, rising to stunning heights (over 300 feet tall) and can survive up to two thousand years. Surprisingly, redwoods have very shallow root systems, only six to twelve feet deep.[1] How can such massive trees survive floods, fires, and earthquakes for hundreds of years without toppling over?

Redwoods survive through underground connections that have been called the "wood-wide web." Though their root systems are shallow, they are wide, spreading out sixty to one hundred feet and intertwining with the roots of other redwoods for stability. Through this intertwining, the trees hold each other up and share energy. They are also connected with each other through underground mycorrhizal fungal networks, sharing water, nutrients, and chemical signals to warn of distress, disease, or insect attacks.[2] These underground connections are a symbiotic relationship between trees and fungi, and for young saplings, this network is essential to their survival. The big trees (the parents) pump sugar into the roots of these young saplings, ensuring their growth and survival. Put another way, this is how mother trees "suckle their young."[3]

The Pando Aspen grove in Utah is considered the largest living organism on earth. All the trees are a single living organism, sharing one root system.[4] What affects one tree in the grove affects the entire community. What lessons we can learn from trees! It reminds me of the quote by Dr. Martin Luther King Jr.: "Injustice anywhere is a threat to justice everywhere. We are caught in an inescapable network of mutuality, tied in a single garment of destiny. Whatever affects one directly, affects all indirectly."[5]

A simple example of this is something I'll call "the casserole network." If an individual has an illness, has a baby, is moving, or experiences a death or loss, the casserole network is put in motion. An online food sign-up list is put together, and meals are dropped off to the person in need. Actually, people don't make casseroles so much anymore (are we all okay with that?), but it's an example of the ecosystem of a community coming together to help someone who could use an extra hand. Now a casserole isn't the same as deep roots, but there is a surface layer at work.

## COLLECTIVE EFFERVESCENCE

When we get close to people and allow space for the sharing of our lives, we experience something like collective effervescence, a "connection, communal emotion, and a 'sensation of sacredness,'" a term coined by French sociologist Émile Durkheim.[6] Durkheim suggested that we experience this when we shift our focus off ourselves, or the individual, and to the group, or community. Researchers later studied and identified these experiences of how "collective assembly" contributes to our lives, offering us a sense of meaning and increased social connection, and assuaging our loneliness.

Collective living is hallowed space. Sharing and listening and giving to one another are affirmations that others are worth our time, they are valued. It is an expression of holiness and the work of belonging. We are modeling what sets us apart as those who love others and the people of this world.

We don't have to fully agree or completely understand one another to validate the humanity of the person sharing. But listening and living in proximity and offering time validate the worth of that other human being. As ethnic minorities, we can listen to each other. We have each other, and we give our stories to each other. We honor this space between us.

We are each on our own journeys of living and healing in spaces that either affirm or do not affirm our presence. I encourage you to find ways to live and share in community. Your close circle, and God, validate you as a person of color with an experience that is valuable and worthy. You do not have to hide. You can make yourself seen and known. You are worthy, your story is worthy, your life and experience are worthy to be shared. In the deliberate decision of God to make you who you are and where you are, your presence, your story, and your voice matter. I resonate with actress and producer Viola Davis's rules about sharing and belonging:

1. I'm doing the best I can.
2. I will allow myself to be seen.

3. Go further. Don't be afraid. Put it all out there. Don't leave anything on the floor.
4. I will not be a mystery to those who love me. She will know me and I will share my story with her—the stories of failure, shame, and accomplishment. She will know she's not alone in the wilderness.

This is who I am.

This is where I am from.

This is my mess.

This is what it means to belong to myself.[7]

*I will allow myself to be seen. I will not be a mystery to those who love me. This is who I am.* I've printed these "rules" out and placed them where I can see them regularly, to remind myself how I want to be in the world.

In Sanskrit, the word *akasha* refers to a collective presence and memory among us, something like community effervescence—or the communal aspects of community.[8] If loneliness spreads like a contagion, so must its opposite: the benefits of being in community also spread. We see this interconnectedness exemplified in the community of trees—and even casserole networks—and we can entertain the possibility that an even more complex chemical web also exists within our community contexts, that there is also unseen physiological as well as spiritual energy at work in our lives.

I don't mean to suggest we possess some sort of clairvoyance that lets us know when a neighbor or friend is in distress or where there might be a friendship connection. But I do mean to suggest we are wired in a way that we were not meant to be alone. The longing to be together is wrapped within the strands of our DNA. Just as we have a spiritual cavity in us that will be filled by something (God), we also have a relational cavity that can only be filled by being in deep relationship with other people. We crave the sustenance and comfort of community and the rich aspects of diversity. There is a kind of synergy when we are together that doesn't exist when we are apart.

The West has largely been influenced by a philosophy of individualism and materialism and the view of manifest destiny. In contrast, the East has a concept of togetherness, of unitedness. We hear echoes of this same concept of unity from Martin Luther King Jr., Mahatma Gandhi, Dorothy Day, Dietrich Bonhoeffer, and other activists, theologians, philosophers, and thinkers through the years. What is preventing us from moving toward deeper community and away from marginalizing ethnic minorities? Perhaps one reason is approval from others. "Human approval is one of our most treasured idols," according to Brown.[9] When we live for someone else's expectations, we end up doing violence to ourselves, to God, and to others, writes Pete Scazzero, author of *Emotionally Healthy Spirituality*.[10] Living authentically means being who we are and knowing who we are, so we bring our healthiest selves.

Another reason we don't move toward a deeper connection with others is fear. We fear difference. We fear what we do not know or understand, and this fear can also be an idol.

Part of living in community is learning to lament in community, acknowledging the sorrow that another member feels and mourning with those who mourn. It is a way of sending along the signals of communal help the way root systems do. By being with others and acknowledging pain, praying together, being together in community with those who need it, we are living in that kind of connected ecosystem. The same holds true for celebrating joyous occasions together. Sharing in collective joy and sorrow is part of living in a community. "Rejoice with those who rejoice; mourn with those who mourn," says the apostle Paul (Rom 12:15).

Sometimes the concept of community is held up as the highest ideal to overcome loneliness. "We have all known the long loneliness and we have learned that the only solution is love and that love comes with community," wrote activist Dorothy Day.[11] Community is indeed vital, and we should and *must* seek authentic community, join small groups, and do life together. But community, though crucial and necessary, is not itself a panacea for our multiple relational deficits. "He who loves his dream of a community more than the Christian community itself becomes a destroyer of the latter" wrote Dietrich Bonhoeffer in his classic volume *Life Together*.[12] Community for its own sake is an idol. Our love for one another supersedes the rest. We are designed for interdependence, like those redwoods and aspens.

## COLLECTIVE CULTURAL MEMORY

A few years ago, I started recording my parents' stories. I'll ask questions, and hit the record button on my phone, letting them share what comes to their mind. I want to preserve and document their stories, their legacy, their homeland, their courage to leave as immigrants, and the years hence for the future—for my children and my children's children. So, I ask for their stories of childhood, what they ate, their daily routine, who their relatives were, and any other memories they want to share, advice they want to leave behind. I want to get to know my parents as they were in another context, in their birth and home country. What do they think about their immigrant life? What were their regrets? What are they happy about? What have they learned from their years of experience? What stories did their parents tell them that they want to pass down? What do they want us, and future generations, to know and remember?

I have more questions than we seem to have time to answer. Answering the questions stirs up more memories. For my mother, in particular, she can feel some of the events as if they were yesterday. She'll talk about Partition and her aunt, and the trauma of those years with tears in her eyes.

One of the more powerful aspects of sharing stories is the sharing of cultural memory. Cultural memory is the "collective knowledge from one generation to the next that gives many of us a chance to reconstruct our cultural identity," writes Kat Armas.[13] If you have the privilege of capturing stories from your parents, grandparents, or other relatives, it is a rich source of cultural wisdom, history, and knowledge. These stories fuel us with courage and offer us a sense of identity, history, and a foundation for the present.

Talking about the past can be complicated. Sometimes, when our own elders aren't able or willing to talk about the past because of painful memories, we can read about it on our own. I realized that whatever I couldn't learn from my parents' stories, I could still glean from history books. It wouldn't be from their perspective, but sometimes I can learn from other historical sources what some of our elders find too painful and difficult to share.

## THE NEIGHBORHOOD

An article in the *Washington Post* explains how suburbs are becoming more diverse, but most people still live in neighborhoods with others who look like them. So while it's getting more diverse, it's still segregated.[14] *Xenophobia* is defined as a fear of people from other countries, foreigners, or those who do not look like us; a fear of "the other."[15] Independence and individualism are associated with an "absence of need."[16] But the truth is we do need each other, though we may act and go on as if we do not. The epidemic of loneliness is proof enough.

I wonder if it's no coincidence that in Japan, people have longer life spans and elderly people are respected and revered as wise. It could be related to diet or lifestyle but also that the elderly know they're valued, wanted, and respected.

My friend Melanie, who lives in DC, shared a story with me about a time she decided to engage in conversation with someone different from herself:

> There's a man named Lance who operates an unlicensed car shop in the alleyway behind my house. Lance and I differ in race, gender, age, and socioeconomic status. Sometimes I'm honestly annoyed by his work, as it increases traffic in the alleyway and can block access to my garage.
>
> One afternoon a couple years ago, I needed to go into my garage to get something while Lance was out back, working on a car. The car's owner was also there, and he was chatting with Lance. I admittedly fought annoyance at that moment, as I just wanted to get on with my day. But I felt led to try to be friendly, so I asked Lance and the customer, "How're you doing?" Turns out, the customer had recently returned from fishing in the Potomac River. The car owner grew up fishing in the Potomac, and was telling me about the fish he can find there, especially an invasive species called the snakehead. Lance and his friend said that the snakehead is really delicious, and they then shared stories about grilling it.
>
> I appreciated that conversation, which not only humanized Lance and his customer for me, but also expanded my sense of awareness (and wonder) about my adopted city of DC. And just a couple months ago, I learned about a restaurant in Baltimore that's serving invasive species, including the snakehead fish! When I learned that, I thought about my conversation with Lance and the fisherman that day.
>
> I doubt Lance and I will be close friends; honestly his work in the alleyway sometimes still irks me. The situation can

feel messy. Yet we've both made efforts to navigate mutually agreeable boundaries for our lives and work, and I've learned that making the effort to have humanizing conversations invites me to step outside of my own life and assumptions. Thankfully Lance is the type of person who will give me a real response when I ask, "How're you doing?" So, I've learned only to ask it when I'm ready to listen, and to have my own life expanded. Lance teaches me how to listen.

I like how Melanie describes how her own life expanded by listening and engaging, and how we become more human to each other. Sometimes we have to turn aside our own annoyance and sometimes we have to make sure we take the time to truly listen. But also, when someone asks, we have the choice of telling them the truth of how it really is.

Our gifts don't lie waiting and fallow. They can be used in spite of what isn't or is going on beyond ourselves. Belonging and self-worth are not defined by those who are excluding us—and we don't have to make the choice to exclude others in our own life in the same way. The fibers of community are in our hands. We are connected to an extensive root system.

## BETWEENNESS IS OUR SUPERPOWER

Vulnerability feels risky. We may walk timidly, afraid to share, to speak up—and even to take up space. When our culture has told us we don't belong and has diminished our experiences as nonexistent, then speaking our stories feels like a bold and dangerous move. But our in-betweenness is what makes our stories powerful. People are thirsty and hungry for stories that are multidimensional and not flattened existences of a single narrative. We are all complex, and storytelling has the power to penetrate the hearts and minds of others. Don't be a mystery to those who love you. Share your life. Armas writes:

> Our histories are complicated, our identities complex. This reality means that our very existence as people of dos mundos (two worlds) is one that resists dominant Western cultures' preference that we fit into colonial dichotomies. The binary of Western culture has simplified our identities, made us into a one-dimensional people, and destroyed what makes us complex. . . . But what if our betweenness is our superpower.[17]

True belonging isn't something we negotiate with the world, like a good or an object. It isn't a transaction. It simply *is*. Diminishing the truth of our own experience or our pain and comparing it with others leads us to being less empathetic with others and ourselves.[18] True belonging is knowing and believing that God made an intentional, deliberate decision with me—to make me the way I am, to place me here, in the culture I live, and that I belong here, as much as anyone else—and God did the same for you, even in this in-between place.

## THE ROLE OF COMMUNITY ORGANIZATIONS AND CHURCHES

How can our community organizations, churches, cultural centers, and support networks work in combating ethnic loneliness? These have a vital role to play in creating places of validation and belonging. Here's how they can contribute:

- *Facilitating social connections.* Organizations and churches can provide places for people to gather and connect with others and share. This reduces isolation and fosters a sense of belonging.

- *Sharing resources.* Organizations can share information, resources, and guidance on various topics relevant to ethnic
  minorities and teach about ethnic loneliness.

- *Cultural preservation.* Cultural centers play a critical role in
  preserving and promoting cultural heritage. Centers can offer
  workshops, educational programs, resources, and activities related to different cultures and ethnicities, and help individuals
  maintain their cultural identities and foster connections with
  their roots.

- *Language and communication support.* Organizations can offer
  language classes, communication support, tutoring, and help with
  immigration questions. Assisting individuals with overcoming
  barriers helps to overcome feelings of isolation. My church has a
  language center that offers English as a Second Language classes
  as well as community and immigration support.

- *Advocacy work.* Organizations can use their collective voice
  to engage in advocacy efforts aimed at addressing systemic inequalities and promoting policies that benefit the
  marginalized.

- *Mentorship and guidance.* Cultural centers, community organizations, and churches can offer mentorship programs, con-
  necting experienced individuals with newcomers to provide
  guidance and support at varying transition points in their
  lives.

- *Promote crosscultural understanding.* Through cultural events,
  workshops, and discussion, these organizations can promote
  understanding between different ethnic groups, breaking
  down stereotypes.

- *Combating discrimination and bias.* Organizations can take active
  steps to address discrimination, bias, and microaggressions,

and create safe spaces for individuals to express themselves without fear of judgment.

- *Supporting families.* Organizations can provide support for families, addressing the challenges faced by children and families in maintaining their cultural identities while integrating into a new culture.

- *Cuisine exploration.* Our organizations and churches can be places to explore various cuisines from around the world. Sharing meals and learning about the cultural significance of different foods foster a sense of connection and camaraderie.

- *Art and music showcases.* Organizing art exhibitions, music concerts, and dance performances that highlight the rich cultural heritage of our communities leads to crosscultural appreciation. Last year I visited an art gallery in Alpharetta, Georgia, which highlighted female artists from India, followed by cultural dance performances. It was an excellent example of this.

- *Cultural storytelling.* Creating forums where individuals can share stories, anecdotes, and experiences related to their cultural heritage helps combat ethnic loneliness and reaches attendees with the power of story.

- *Collaborative projects.* Organizations can come together to collaborate on community projects that celebrate cultural diversity, such as mural painting, community gardens, or public art installations.

- *Intergenerational sharing.* Facilitating interactions between different generations within a community allows for the passing down of cultural knowledge and traditions, while strengthening ties between diverse age groups.

- *Crosscultural dialogues.* Organizing panel discussions or dialogues where individuals can share their perspectives and experiences related to cultural diversity fosters understanding and empathy.

- *Conflict resolution training.* Organizations can offer training in conflict resolution techniques that can help us address misunderstandings and disagreements in a constructive manner.

- *Interfaith dialogues.* Churches can come together to promote understanding and foster connection by hosting interfaith meals or dialogues.

- *Community-wide prayer events.* Churches can lead efforts in bringing the community together in times of prayer and lament, fostering connection and meeting the spiritual needs of the community, especially to engage in prayer on behalf of marginalized and ethnic communities.

- *Cultural awareness events.* Organizations can launch awareness campaigns that highlight the importance of cultural and ethnic diversity.

- *Supporting minority-owned businesses.* This helps the community and contributes to economic empowerment.

Celebrating our cultural diversity is a powerful tool in combating ethnic loneliness. Fostering connections, promoting understanding, and providing support help ethnic minorities find a sense of belonging. These help promote social connection, too, which is a determining factor in loneliness. Building bridges between ethnic groups requires intentional effort and a commitment and desire to acknowledge and address the impacts of ethnic loneliness.

As ethnic minorities, we can participate in this work by supporting and encouraging these efforts and one another. We can support each other by listening and learning from one another, building personal relationships with each other, showing compassion for one another, sharing our cultural experiences with each other, advocating for inclusion for one another, being respectful of our differences, asking questions with respect, being allies for each other, and showing solidarity during difficult times. As ethnic minorities, these are ways we can help each other in combating ethnic loneliness.

## A PLEASING AROMA

The aromatic scent of spices, garlic, onions, cumin seeds, and garam masala cooking on the stove reminds me of my mother's cooking. The scent of mothballs whisks me back to a large heavy metal trunk from India, where my mother stored handmade Indian textiles. Of the five senses, smell is the strongest and most evocative, spiraling us through time and space, eliciting memories that no other sense can. We are comforted by certain scents, but describing scent is an elusive task. Indeed, how does one describe the smell of freshly baked bread, the scent of a peeled banana, or the aroma of a rose or freshly cut grass?

A scent disperses in a space as its molecules diffuse from a place of higher concentration to lower concentration. If you spritz perfume in one corner of a room, soon the aroma will diffuse all over the room. In Exodus, Leviticus, and Numbers we read that our prayers are like incense, a pleasing aroma to God, "'reah nihoah,' a soothing odor."[19] Our prayers diffuse across time and space, across dimensions, from the physical to the spiritual realm to reach God's nose. God can smell our prayers.

Loneliness, as mentioned previously, has been described as a contagion, spreading through social networks like a cold, with invisible molecules diffusing across our physical space. Is there such a chemical for loneliness too? That isn't to say it's like a microbe, and we must wear masks to prevent "catching" it. But studies indicate that lonely people share their loneliness with others, and move to the edges of social networks, likening it to a contagion, or a "yarn that comes loose at the end of a crocheted sweater."[20]

Indeed, sometimes sadness and anger feel palpable in a room. Have you ever felt the sorrow or joy of another human being or the energy in a room when a particular person enters? Our bodies communicate with more than what we speak or write or gesticulate. Anger and anxiety also spread, just like the scent of a perfume, in an imperceptible way.

Horses can distinguish between positive and negative human facial expressions and can sense emotion.[21] In the plant kingdom, mushrooms communicate with one another using electrical impulses, through their hyphae, sharing information about food and injury.[22] Trees are linked together by a complex underground fungi network, resembling the brain's neural network, and send chemical signals to one another, warning of danger.[23]

I have to admit if someone around me is in tears, it's hard for me to hold back my own. Emerging neuroscience is confirming the fact that our emotions are contagious.[24] Anger and anxiety are contagious. Smiles and yawns are contagious. We must have imperceptible chemical olfactory signals to communicate with one another of our loneliness, too, for this emotion cluster, though we have not yet isolated it. And perhaps, even before we have words in our biological vocabulary or textbooks, might we be able to deflect some of it, to assuage the ache of loneliness, to stop its spread?

I wonder what the scent of community might be. What aroma describes the scent of belonging? What is the fragrance for a longing for something in the future but not yet realized? If we were to find the opposite of loneliness—what I am naming as belonging—what pleasing fragrance would result? Is belonging as contagious as loneliness? My contention is that yes, even more so.

The opposite agents are kindness, love, acts of goodness—which we also know to be contagious.

If we were all born looking for a face, with the longing of someone to know us, then this longing must have an answer. We are a pleasing aroma to God (2 Cor 2:15). *We are an aroma.* Our words, both the spoken and unspoken, and our presence have a fragrance, like incense, reaching all the way to heaven (Rev 8:4). Likewise, living in beloved community is a beautiful fragrance that embodies love and draws others in. Can we imagine what the fragrance of multiethnic community could be, drawing others in?

• • •

We live in a world of multiple ethnicities with a multitude of stories. True community is finding safe spaces where we can be ourselves, and the freedom and courage we acquire from that place nourishes us, giving us the courage to step beyond ourselves to listen to those who are not like us. We've allowed pieces of our identities to get stolen, and that means others miss out on a diversity of perspective and living in multiethnic, beloved community. It impacts the entire community as it was meant to be. Our longing is a divine longing. This yearning for a sense of togetherness, a belonging together, is what we were meant for.

If we have no peace because we do not belong to each other, then it follows our peace will be restored when we remind ourselves of this belonging to one another and align ourselves toward this goal. Peace isn't independence or homogeneity. It's found in interdependence.

## SO, WHAT ARE YOU?

You are not an isolated
Human being

You belong to all the people
You see around you
And they belong
To you
You are part of me
And I am part of you
Don't be a mystery
We are keepers of multiple stories
We are keepers of each other
And we are all learning
How to be human
Moment by moment
One day at a time

## QUESTIONS FOR REFLECTION AND DISCUSSION

1. How do you interact with the idea of community and loneliness? Do you feel a sense of interdependence or independence?

2. Writing prompts:
   - "I get my power from . . ."
   - "My community's strength is . . ."

3. What specific activities do you sense an immediate need for in your own community or place of worship? Are there one or two from the list in this chapter that resonate with you?

# 10

# A BETTER COUNTRY

*Our goal is to create a beloved community.*

Martin Luther King Jr.

*Where is the door to God?*
*In the sound of a barking dog,*
*In the ring of a hammer,*
*In a drop of rain,*
*In the face of*
*Everyone*
*I see.*

Daniel Ladinsky,
inspired by
poet Hafez of Shiraz

When my son Josh was a preteen, he walked door to door in the neighborhood, asking if anyone needed their grass mowed. Through that endeavor, he met an elderly Ukrainian Jewish neighbor in his nineties, who was homebound and lived alone. That was the beginning of a years-long friendship between my son and this neighbor, a person we didn't even know existed until that point. My son visited Mr. B regularly and listened to his stories, and I joined him on occasion. When we asked him how he was doing,

he'd respond with a smile, and say, "Oh, I'm just schlepping along!"
He had a sense of humor and cheerful disposition despite his dif-
ficulty hearing, lack of mobility, pain, and other health issues. Yet
he still managed to get dressed every day, greet us with a smile, and
always had a joke or two. Our visits were brief because he couldn't
handle long visits, but they were meaningful.

Mr. B loved to talk about politics, and he remembered stories
as if they had happened yesterday, which impressed me immensely
because I have trouble remembering what I ate yesterday for lunch.
Mr. B had lost an adult son, survived an earthquake in California, and
lost his wife. He lived a fascinating and long life and was proud of the
fact that he had brought the first quick oil change service business to
the city. He could talk about almost any subject, kept a large stack of
books nearby, and was always learning something new as he occupied
himself during the long monotonous days by reading. At his age,
most of his friends had passed away. He did have a caregiver come
to the house, and enjoyed visits by his children, so he wasn't always
alone, but he spent much time in solitude, reading books or napping.

One year near Christmas, Mr. B remarked how pretty Christmas
trees looked from the outside as he drove by other people's homes
(he still drove until the last couple of years of his life). I invited
Mr. B over to our house for lunch a few days later to look at our
Christmas tree and he accepted. I researched kosher cooking and
made a dish of kosher fried rice for the occasion. He liked it so
much he asked me for the recipe, and then he ended up making
fried rice several times for his Sabbath supper, a tradition which he
still kept with his adult children every Friday night. Who would
have guessed that our Jewish neighbor would make Indian-style
fried rice for his weekly Sabbath?

Mr. B enjoyed our Christmas tree and decorations, and he
pointed to a piece of artwork I had, which has 1 Corinthians 13

written in beautiful calligraphy with golden and colored ink. He read it and asked me about it, and when I told him where it came from, he said, "Oh, that's from the Bible. You see, there's good things from the Bible." Then he talked about the Jewish Scriptures and connections to the Bible.

Mr. B had a rabbi who would come visit him once a week, and they'd discuss issues, the Torah, and life in general. My son would attend on occasion, whenever he could, because he wanted to learn and be part of their discussion.

Mr. B, a Ukrainian Jewish businessman, and my son, a South Asian Christian teenager, would not have met were it not for a door-knocking preteen looking for a summer job. While I would like to tell you the motives were to make a crosscultural friendship, that is not the case—the original plan was a desire for a summer job, but a friendship is exactly what happened, and it started by a knock on a neighbor's door. One Friday evening, we received a phone call from Mr. B's caregiver that he had become seriously ill and was taken to a hospice facility. We visited him the next morning. He was asleep most of the time because of his medication, but he woke up for a few minutes, and in typical Mr. B style, he welcomed us and graciously thanked us for the visit, as he always had done when we went to his house.

Mr. B passed away that same night, at the age of 102. We were invited to the ceremony at his house and the shiva at his daughter's home. It was an honor to be invited—and we felt as if we belonged to the inner circle surrounding a dear friend. The times spent with Mr. B were a special memory for our family. Our friendship made the world feel a little less lonely. He always appreciated our visits, and we appreciated him. No matter what we discussed, even if we didn't agree, Mr. B was kind and generous and eager to talk. I wish we had more people like Mr. B in this world. My son was the closest to him, and grieved the most, but we all loved our dear neighbor and have a Mr. B hole in our lives.

We live surrounded by people who are both like us and unlike us. Different perspectives add richness to life. We are incomplete without acknowledging the "other." If racial and ethnic homogeneity had been part of the Creator's design, we'd be living in a very different world.

In my own story of unbecoming, then becoming, I could only be complete when I reconciled with this identity I had left behind, the person who was not just part of me; she *was me*. God was there, guiding me on the path to wholeness and restoration. It wasn't just me, but God's love opening the way to seeing myself as beloved, as wanted, as known, as seen. And God sees you that way too.

Healing came when I learned that I didn't have to live in an either/or existence but rather as a person who lives in a both/and reality. I am not one or the other but *both*. I don't have to choose one piece of myself and neglect the other. Otherwise, I am a scattered jigsaw puzzle, constantly dropping and picking up pieces and trying to put myself together. Embracing all the different parts of who I am makes me whole. Belonging isn't exclusive to one space.

God says we belong and adopts us. Instead of being the perpetual foreigner, we are perpetually known, seen, and loved. Even in those times of life when I felt invisible, othered, marginalized, and like I didn't belong, I found healing in finally accepting and celebrating my ethnic identity and culture. Regardless of the dominant cultural view of us and regardless of the oppressive systems in place, the reality of who we are and what God thinks remains the same. There's hope and healing in that knowledge. It means that our security and sense of belonging is found in an unchangeable source. It doesn't mean we're doormats or that we must stay silent. It means we can be confident and take up space and use our voice.

## THE GIFTS OF LONELINESS

Perhaps our loneliness is how we can find one another again. Kristen Radtke in *Seek You* ends her book about loneliness with the words "I want us to use loneliness—yours, and mine—to find our way back to each other."[1] If loneliness is the condition of our modern age, then we can follow its lead back to God, back to each other, and back to ourselves.

As we identify with the marginalized and the unseen, we realize that Jesus wasn't seen or known either. He was constantly misunderstood. Repeatedly rejected. As our roots go deep in God, we also become aware of the unseen things of God. God exhorts us to look at the unseen and be at work in the seen world.[2] As people who have lived as unseen, marginalized, isolated, othered, we can represent what is unseen to a hurting world: that is, that hope exists, that God's love is available, that God created each of us and our unique identities. We can share our lives and our stories. The minds, hearts, and hands of those around us are hungry for—and need—these stories.

As Austin Channing Brown reminds us in her memoir *I'm Still Here*, steps toward change are not usually the effort of millions of people, but just a *few transformed* "people of color confronting past and present to imagine a new future, and the handful of white people willing to release indifference and join the struggle."[3] While the factors that lead toward lasting cultural change are multifaceted and sometimes beyond our control, it's important we never forget how God can use just a few transformed people.

Although loneliness feels difficult to talk about, we can normalize it. We're afraid of people judging us for it, or worried what others will think, when those around us are dying of the same condition. We can address this in our society before it becomes an even more destructive and debilitating condition than it already is. Our ethnic loneliness is nothing to be ashamed of. It is a sign that something is amiss. That doesn't mean there is something amiss with me, or you, or our faith. It means something is broken in our world. David Whyte writes, "Loneliness is the place from which we pay real attention to voices other than our own; being alone allows us to find the healing power in the other."[4] Loneliness wakes me up to the need for others. Loneliness is a force pulling me out of myself.

Living in places of aloneness and othering gives us the gift of empathy and understanding. We live our lives. We take up space. In ways we find congruent with our personalities and circumstances, we can speak up for those who cannot speak for themselves, and we can speak up against systems and institutions that continue to oppress the marginalized and weak. The question of our age is always, How am I going to respond? And more specifically, How am I going to respond to the ethnic loneliness in my life and of those around me?

By embracing the gifts learned in ethnic loneliness, we can move that much closer to others. Ethnic loneliness is a gift that might stay attached to us like spiny burrs we are constantly running into and trying to remove. But it is more than a thorn. Thorns suggest the presence of a rose, and our loneliness is a fragrance drawing us, and others, closer in. Ethnic loneliness:

- points to our need for God
- points to our need for each other
- points to the need to live authentically with ourselves and our convictions, with who God designed and made us to be
- shows us we are all part of the same family, no matter our ethnicity, race, culture, background, or skin color

## HAVE YOU EATEN?

Asian mothers around the world are known for asking, "Have you eaten?" If we could gather our Asian mothers and grandmothers in one giant potluck, we'd all be fed well. Reminding each other to eat is one way of showing love to one another in ethnic communities, especially by well-intentioned, caring, zealous moms and grandmas practically shoving food down our throats. Eating food in other cultures is a meaningful experience, even a ritual, an act that develops community and relational bonds. In the United States, we tend to see food as a means of staving off hunger, instead of lingering over meals and enjoying conversation and bonding together. This is one of the gifts our multicultural communities can bring to cultures that value expediency and rely on superficial transactions, to help them understand community and hospitality.

Sherene, an Indian American who immigrated from India, had a good friend who once admitted she was disgusted by the smell and taste of Indian food. It took Sherene by surprise, and she didn't know how to respond. To integrate our cultures and experiences, we need to be willing to try something new, even if we don't think we'd like it. Thinking about all the meals that Jesus ate in other people's homes, do you think Jesus would have eaten biryani? Kimchi? I can't imagine Jesus saying, "Um, no, I'm not used to that. It smells awful! Just give me a few olives, a piece of fish freshly caught from the Sea of Galilee, and a piece of bread, please." It's kind of laughable, isn't it? Food and eating are part of being human. We have to eat, and sharing meals together is an important way people spend time in community, all across the world. As Eugene Peterson once said, "We don't become more spiritual by becoming less human."[5] Breaking bread and sharing meals together is one of many ways we find a sense of belonging and share our humanness.

In many parts of the world, extending and showing hospitality is a serious matter. In India, there is a saying, *atithi devo bhav*, meaning "guests are forms of God." People in India give guests the highest regard. It doesn't mean they worship their guests, but they treat them with respect and honor. When I was in India, I noticed people—strangers—willing to help others out, in various forms and ways. An elderly woman couldn't walk upstairs in a particular building, so a group of strangers came together and carried her up the stairs while she was seated in a chair. Scenarios like this are repeated time and again. "Do not forget to show hospitality to strangers, for by so doing some people have shown hospitality to angels without knowing it" (Heb 13:2). The word *hospitality* here is the Greek word *philoxenia*, which is the opposite of *xenophobia*. It is derived from *xenos*, which means something like "stranger" or "foreigner," and *philos*, which means something like "friend" or "love."[6]

In the Old Testament, the story of Boaz and Ruth describes this hospitality. In their day, wheat threshers and gatherers were told to leave behind stalks of wheat for the poor who'd come later and gather for themselves. In this way, provision was made during the harvest to help others in need. Boaz was a wealthy man who followed Yahweh, and Ruth was a Moabite, from another land. After both Ruth and her mother-in-law, Naomi, became widowed, Ruth followed Naomi, traveling back to Bethlehem. When Ruth and Naomi came upon Boaz's land, Boaz inquired who Ruth belonged to, and he showed compassion and kindness on Ruth and Naomi, both vulnerable, by permitting Ruth to glean in his fields and stay close to the women workers. Boaz spoke kindly to Ruth, went above and beyond the usual hospitality by offering her water, and invited her to share a meal with his reapers. Ruth acknowledged she was "a foreigner" (Ruth 2:10). She was fully aware she was a Moabite, and pondered the kindness and generosity of Boaz. It just so happened that Boaz was a relative of Ruth's husband who had passed away, and as part of God's remarkable plan, Boaz married Ruth.

Hospitality is a valued component of Arab culture as well. Arab hospitality, called *karam*, is more than simply just offering food and drink. It's a deeply embedded sense of honor:

> "A house without guests, without the spaces necessary to take them in, and without the materials needed to prepare food and drink, is not only weak, it is shameful." Hospitality is a kind of deep faith there, ... "'a burning in the skin' inherited 'from the father and the grandfathers.'". . . "*Karam* is not just a matter of food and drink. Hospitality is from the soul; it's from the blood."[7]

*From the soul, from the blood.* This is stunning. I learned from my parents a different level of hospitality, which is one that gives in abundance. My parents make sure to have plenty of food and give the gift of time and provisions. For my parents, for example, not having enough seats at the dinner table wouldn't be seen as an obstacle for not having guests. If there is no table or chairs, they'll toss some cushions on the floor, and there's space for you—and this is true for many other cultures as well.

In India, it is not at all unusual for neighbors and family and friends to stop by without notice, and when invited for a meal, it is customary to bring the host or hostess a gift. My mind is filled with memories of shoes left by the door by guests—this is the custom for many households from Asia and other countries. When my siblings and I visit our parents, my mother gives us fruit, loaves of banana bread, and any other leftover food she has, putting it in bags and placing it in our hands.

Japan has a tradition called *omotenashi*, which translates to "spirit of service." It is grounded in the ritual of sado, the tea ceremony, which involves attentiveness on the part of the host, fulfilling the needs of the guest without expecting anything in return. This is actually a way of life in Japan, with shop and restaurant workers bowing to guests and patrons, taxi drivers opening doors. But what is especially fascinating is they offer an even higher level of politeness to foreigners or to those outside their group.[8] For many other cultures around the world, treating a guest or strangers well is a matter of honor.

## ABIGAIL SAVES THE DAY

First Samuel 25 tells the story of a beautiful and intelligent woman named Abigail. She was married to a wealthy man named Nabal, who owned some land and animals in the Middle East. One day, Nabal was out with his men shearing sheep. David (the future king) and his men came upon Nabal's property and animals, and protected his property from thieves. David later politely asked Nabal for some food. It was a feasting season, and this sort of hospitality was considered typical for that culture. Nabal was known to be harsh and instead of offering food, scoffed at David.

David was livid, and he and his four hundred men began sharpening their swords and planned to attack that very evening and kill every male in the household. A servant rushed to give this news to Abigail, Nabal's wife, and openly referred to Nabal as a "scoundrel." Abigail didn't deny or argue with the servant. She believed him. This whole exchange proves Abigail was trusted among the household staff and that Nabal obviously had an unfavorable reputation in his household.

Abigail leaped into action and dispatched orders for large quantities of food and provisions to be loaded on donkeys and delivered to David, all without Nabal's knowledge. Abigail's got some gumption and smarts.

When Abigail neared David, she fell on her face and humbly begged for forgiveness for the foolishness of Nabal. She called

Nabal a scoundrel too. She pleaded for the lives of her household and encouraged David not to seek revenge and create bloodshed, and asked him to accept her gifts. She acknowledged David as the future king, recounting the stories she had heard about his battles.

The last thing David expected to see were donkeys laden with food and a gesture of humility and request for forgiveness. What did he do? David conceded. He confessed that he would have killed each male in her house, thanked Abigail for keeping him from bloodshed, and thanked God for her intervention. No one could convince Nabal to share his food, but Abigail could convince David not to murder all the men in her household. Some folks are harder to reason with than others!

When Abigail returned that evening, Nabal was hosting a feast fit for a king and very drunk. The next morning, Abigail told Nabal what happened, and he ended up having a stroke or heart attack and died ten days later. As fast as news could travel back then, David heard that Nabal had died, and now, David acted fast. I think Abigail knocked his socks off (or sandals?), because he sent a proposal right out to Abigail, asking her to marry him, and she said yes. The tradition of hospitality is taken seriously.

Hospitality is one gift we have to offer. But we have more. We have diverse strengths in our communities, and we offer multiple and unique perspectives that enrich the lives of society. This diversity is a source of strength. Our skills contribute to culture in a myriad of ways. But—here's the thing—while this is true, our value isn't only or solely in what we bring. Our value is already inherent in *who we are*.

Paul writes, "There is neither Jew nor Gentile, neither slave nor free, nor is there male and female, for you are all one in Christ Jesus" (Gal 3:28). We are all one in Christ. There is no caste system, no hierarchy based on colorism or race. We are all parts of one body, and these parts form one body (the human race) (1 Cor 12:12-13). And what is required of us? "To act justly and to love mercy and to walk humbly with your God" (Mic 6:8). Scripture tells us we are one body; we are to walk humbly, love mercy, and act justly; and we are to love one another (Jn 13:34-35).

## A BETTER COUNTRY

Have you found your ghost self? Your lost or stolen identity? The parts of yourself that were fragmented, left behind, forgotten in your struggle to live authentically and true? It's possible to live holistically and completely and fully, even amid the tensions we experience in society. We can put our sights on a "better country." There is a better country that exists, that awaits. In a practical sense, it's where we are right now, and it's a place we look forward to:

> All these people died in faith without receiving the promises, but they saw the promises from a distance and welcomed them. They confessed that they were strangers and immigrants on earth. People who say this kind of thing make it clear that they are looking for a homeland. If they had been thinking about the country that they had left, they would have had the opportunity to return to it. But at this point in time, they are longing for a better country, that is, a heavenly one. Therefore, God isn't ashamed to be called their God—he has prepared a city for them. (Heb 11:13-16 CEB)

In the Beatitudes (Mt 5), Jesus turns the world order upside down. He tells us the kingdom is for the meek, the weak, the powerless, the thirsty, those who mourn, and the peacemakers. The ideas of kingdom have nothing to do with notions of race, wealth, military power, or status. The kingdom is characterized by Christlikeness; that is to say, by mercy, by love, by humility.

Maybe the land we live in will take long to change. We continue to press on, sharing ourselves and our stories, and loving our neighbors, no matter their ethnicity or race, and keeping our healthy boundaries in place. Maybe we'll find, as we live our days, pockets of belonging that eluded us before, as we remember that the loneliness we experience shows us the need for companionship. Our loneliness opens up something inside us. It brings us to a spacious place, a land of abundance with the beauty of acceptance and inclusion—starting with ourselves. We hope and aim for a better country now and we know a better one yet awaits.

## YOUR ETHNICITY IS SACRED

When Paul says there is neither Jew nor Greek, it doesn't mean one ethnicity is better than the other or there are extra privileges or points with God (Gal 3:28-29). Jesus isn't a destroyer of culture but a redeemer of culture and ethnicity.[9] Your ethnicity is sacred. Your in-betweenness is holy ground. Honor that space. Your ethnicity is beauty, a letter of love, a welcoming space.

Learn from your ethnic loneliness. Learn how to be alone in it, dive in it, soak in it, celebrate it. Invite others to a feast, to a celebration of ethnic identity. We can love recklessly from this place of belonging, this place of knowing. We can love others in this world as we were designed. The better country is within you and me, and in a place not yet realized. Loneliness doesn't have to be a desolate place—it's an entryway to a place of belonging, not a locked door leading to solitary confinement.

We can go to those who love us. We can make room and space for those who want to love us and invite us in. We can allow others to ask us the question, *Have you eaten?* Have you eaten this feast that celebrates who you are and how you are made, you in your beautiful skin, with your eyes that kiss in the corners,[10] with hair that is wild and curly? You have a place, with yourself, with others, with God, with community, with your place of worship, and with the global body of people. You are a perfectly planned person. Taste the bread of belonging, where nourishment is sweet.

How do you want to be in this world? How do you want to be remembered? For me, it's being who I am. Those who welcome me to do that are essentially saying to me, *Have you eaten?* It's the people who've come into my life and encouraged me to embrace my culture, heritage, background, and who I am—and who accept me as a friend, no matter of that or anything else. *That* is eating at the table of belonging.

You bring the blessing of who you are in the spaces you inhabit, leaving a fragrance of belovedness behind you and around you, touching those who surround you. The world needs your presence, your healing touch, your perspective, your stories, your friendship, your joy, your love. The world isn't the same without you in it. There is no medicine more healing, no force more powerful, than love, and your love is essential. Our ethnicity is a form of medicine for a hurting world. If God didn't think the world needed our multiple ethnicities, we wouldn't be here. We have the opportunity to turn around and ask others the same question: *Have you eaten, beloved?*

So, what are you? You are beloved. You are beloved by a God who knows the composition of each and every living cell in your body, who knows the number of hairs on your head, who painted the pigment on your skin. This God, who calls you beloved, says you belong and beckons you in an embrace. This God is calling you to invite your fragmented and exiled self back home. In all of your places of exile, in all of your wanderings, in all of your questions, your doubts, your isolation, your loneliness, know that you are be-loved. Your ethnic loneliness, your in-between places, your places of exile, are pathways to belonging. Your ethnic loneliness doesn't mark you as a foreigner. It marks you as a citizen of a Beautiful and Spacious Land. This God is calling you home, where you will always belong.

## SO, WHAT ARE YOU?

You are beloved
You are not invisible
You are whole
You are wanted
You are seen
You are loved
Just the way you are
You belong to yourself
You belong to others
You belong to God
So, what are you?
You are a gift of joy
You eat at the table
Of belonging
You are a Home
Of belonging
To others
And yourself

## QUESTIONS FOR REFLECTION AND DISCUSSION

1. What does belonging in a "better country" mean to you? Write or explain what that looks and feels like. Name that country. Perhaps it could be "Land of Abundant Joy" or "Place of Rest" or "Home of Rest" or "Where I Am Known."

2. Writing prompt: "The better country is . . ."

3. Do you see your ethnicity as sacred? Explain.

4. Write your own "So, What Are You?" poem, like the ones at the end of each chapter.

# ACKNOWLEDGMENTS

This book would not be possible without the dreams and courage of immigrants, including my parents. Thank you for your sacrifice and support, Mom and Dad.

Thank you to my children, Natalie, Joshua, and Elijah, who are my delight and joy, who keep me smiling, laughing, and hopeful.

I am also so grateful for the following people:

My amazing editor, Al Hsu, for believing in me and this project, for your wise guidance, and for the staff at InterVarsity Press for your welcome and kindness to a new writer.

My agent, Barb Roose, for saying yes and believing.

My IVP writer friends Susan Lim and Alastair Sterne for your encouragement, support, and feedback, and to Alastair for reading the manuscript and providing incisive feedback. It's been a joy to share words with you both.

Michelle Van Loon and Marlena Graves for your writing class and very early proposal feedback (it's a stretch to call that early mess a proposal, but you were kind). I'm grateful for you and your examples of literary citizenship and integrity. You are bright lights.

Margot Starbuck (you are a rock star) for proposal guidance and development—it is because of you that the proposal got whipped into shape.

Sarah Guerrero for your support, encouragement, and Voxer messages.

Catherine McNeil for not only proposal feedback but also your editing expertise on very early chapter drafts and your general commiseration. You're a neighbor I'd like to have.

Jodi Grubbs for co-writing sessions, Voxer messages, IG messages, feedback, and swapping a chapter or two. You made my days brighter and were one of my go-tos on this journey.

Katie Rose Rouse for making it through a very rough early draft and providing feedback. I don't know how you put up with it, but I'm thankful you did.

Stephanie Lai for feedback on an early version, and Nineesha Koshy for surviving the reading of a very early chapter.

Micha Boyett for feedback on an early chapter that helped set the tone.

My sisters at the Redbud Writers Guild for your support and friendship through the years. I couldn't have done this without you.

My sisters in *The Mudroom* who provide a welcome space of belonging for women writers. Much love to you all.

Marie Chan for your support, kindness, bouncing off ideas, and sharing the writing journey; I'm grateful.

Dorcas Cheng-Tozun for talking with me about books and surveys and writing.

Erin Lane, for your sharp eye in feedback and editing.

Melanie Weldon-Soiset for your friendship and support, for poetry talks and writing talks.

All the families of the Salt & Light speech and debate club that I've had the pleasure of knowing. My time with you has formed me in unforgettable ways, and I am grateful.

My Be the Bridge group for monthly talks and discussions and openly sharing your stories. I learned from you.

The F+J cohort for all of your Asianness and for being you. I appreciated being with you and hearing from you.

The Collegeville Institute, for your care and cultivation for the life of writers, for top-notch workshops and leaders, and for providing space and time to write, think, create, learn, and be. My life is not the same.

Local writing friends, Kendra Broekhuis, Sarah White, Margaret Philbrick, for the meetups, co-writing sessions, and friendship.

Jill Ng for being a supportive writing friend from early on.

My local book club for your willingness to talk about books—and everything else! I wouldn't have it any other way and count myself blessed to be in proximity with you.

Jim Mumm, Sharon Mumm, and the Marquette Law Library for help with research.

Brian Allain, your Publishing in Color conferences provided a way to meet and connect with writers and publishing professionals and paved the way for this book.

My dear friend Lisa Sinclair for your friendship, encouragement, support, and the Marco Polos.

My dear friend Stephanie Todd, who teaches me what it means to be a friend who is there, who asks, who persists, and who has supported me in my life as well as this book project. Thank you for asking, for making time, and for being who you are. You are a gift.

To all those willing to share their stories in this book and for those who completed the survey, you and your stories are a treasure.

# Appendix A

## BIPOC MENTAL HEALTH RESOURCES

**Asian Mental Health Collective**
www.asianmhc.org/
Twitter: @asianmhc
Instagram: @asianmentalhealthcollective
Facebook: @asianmentalhealthcollective

**Asians for Mental Health**
www.asiansformentalhealth.com/
Instagram @Asiansformentalhealth

**The AAKOMA Project**
https://aakomaproject.org/
Twitter: @AAKOMAProject
Instagram: @aakomaproject

**Black Girls Smile**
https://campsite.bio/blackgirlssmile
Twitter: @BlackGirlsSmile
Instagram: @blackgirlssmile

**Brown Girl Therapy**
https://sahajkohli.com/
Twitter: @SahajKohli
Instagram: @browngirltherapy

**Black Mental Wellness**
www.blackmentalwellness.com/
Twitter: @wellnessblack
Instagram: @blackmentalwellness

**National Latino Behavioral Health Association**
https://nlbha.org/
Twitter: @NLBHAORG
Instagram: @nlbhaorg

**South Asian Therapists**
https://southasiantherapists.org/
Twitter: @southasianther1
Instagram: @southasiantherapists

**Therapy for Black Girls**
https://therapyforblackgirls.com/
Twitter: @therapy4bgirls
Instagram: @therapyforblackgirls

**Therapy for Black Men**
https://therapyforblackmen.org/
Twitter: @therapy4blkmen
Instagram: @therapyforblkmen

**Christian Asian American Counselors**
https://camh.network/counselors/

**We R Native**
https://www.wernative.org/
Twitter: @weRnative
Instagram: @wernative

## Melanin and Mental Health

www.melaninandmentalhealth.com/

Twitter: @MelaninHealth

Instagram: @melaninandmentalhealth

## The Nap Ministry

https://thenapministry.com/

Twitter: @TheNapMinistry

Instagram: @thenapministry

## The Loveland Foundation

https://thelovelandfoundation.org/

Instagram: @thelovelandfoundation

## Inclusive Therapists

www.inclusivetherapists.com/

Twitter: @InclusiveMH

Instagram: @inclusivetherapists

## Latinxtherapy

https://latinxtherapy.com/

Twitter: @latinxtherapy

Instagram: @latinxtherapy

# Appendix B

# FURTHER READING

## NONFICTION

*Abuelita Faith*, Kat Armas

*After Whiteness: An Education in Belonging*, Willie James Jennings

*All About Love*, bell hooks

*All the Colors We Will See*, Patrice Gopo

*All the White Friends I Couldn't Keep*, Andre Henry

*Amusing Ourselves to Death*, Neil Postman

*Anam Cara*, John O'Donohue

*The Art of Gathering*, Priya Parker

*Asian American Histories of the United States*, Catherine Ceniza Choy

*Be the Bridge*, Latasha Morrison

*Belonging*, Geoffrey L. Cohen

*Beyond Colorblind*, Sarah Shin

*Beyond Welcome*, Karen González

*A Biography of Loneliness*, Fay Bound Alberti

*Boundaries for Your Soul*, Alison Cook and Kimberly Miller

*Braving the Wilderness*, Brené Brown

*Brown Church*, Robert Chao Romero

*A Brown Girl's Epiphany*, Aurelia Dávila Pratt

*Caste*, Isabel Wilkerson

*The Color of Compromise*, Jemar Tisby

*The Cross and the Lynching Tree*, James Cone

*The Deeply Formed Life*, Rich Villodas

*Fearing Bravely*, Catherine McNeil

*The God Who Sees*, Karen González

*Healing Racial Trauma*, Sheila Wise Rowe

*The Heart of Racial Justice*, Brenda Salter McNeil and Rick Richardson

*A Hidden Wholeness*, Parker Palmer

*The Holy Longing*, Ronald Rolheiser

*How to Be an Antiracist*, Ibram Kendi

*How to Heal Our Divides*, edited by Brian Allain

*I Bring the Voices of My People*, Chanequa Walker-Barnes

*I'm Still Here*, Austin Channing Brown

*Inalienable*, Eric Costanzo, Daniel Yang, and Matthew Soerens

*The Invisible Kingdom*, Meghan O'Rourke

*Jesus and John Wayne*, Kristin Kobes Du Mez

*Learning Our Names*, Sabrina Chan, Linson Daniel, E. David de Leon, and La Thao

*Life Together*, Dietrich Bonhoeffer

*The Life We're Looking For*, Andy Crouch

*The Loneliness Epidemic*, Susan Mettes

*Love Without Limits*, Jacqueline Bussie

*The Making of Asian America*, Erika Lee

*Man's Search for Meaning*, Viktor Frankl

*Many Colors*, Soong-Chan Rah

*The Minority Experience*, Adrian Pei

*Misreading Scripture with Western Eyes*, E. Randolph Richards and Brandon J. O'Brien

*Mixed Blessing*, Chandra Crane

*My Grandmother's Hands*, Resmaa Menakem

*The Pain We Carry*, Natalie Gutierrez

*The Path Out of Loneliness*, Mark Mayfield

*Permission to Come Home*, Jenny Wang

*Race and Place*, David P. Leong

*Racial Melancholia, Racial Dissociation*, David L. Eng and Shinhee Han

*Raise Your Voice*, Kathy Khang

*Saving Grace*, Kristen Powers

*See No Stranger*, Valarie Kaur

*Seek You*, Kristen Radtke

*So You Want to Talk About Race*, Ijeoma Oluo

*Social Justice for the Sensitive Soul*, Dorcas Cheng-Tozun

*A Sojourner's Truth*, Natasha Sistrunk Robinson

*The Soul of Desire*, Curt Thompson

*Southbound: Essays on Identity, Inheritance, and Social Change*, Anjali Enjeti

*Start with Hello*, Shannan Martin

*Suffering and the Heart of God*, Diane Langberg

*Together*, Vivek Murthy

*Uninvited*, Lysa TerKeurst

*The Warmth of Other Suns*, Isabel Wilkerson

*Welcoming the Stranger*, Matthew Soerens and Jenny Yang

*The Wild Edge of Sorrow*, Francis Weller
*The Wisdom of Your Body*, Hillary McBride
*You Are Not Your Own*, Alan Noble

## FICTION, POETRY, MEMOIR

*All You Can Ever Know*, Nicole Chung
*An Asian American A to Z*, Cathy Linh Che and Kyle Lucia Wu
*Beloved*, Toni Morrison
*Born a Crime*, Trevor Noah
*Brown Girl Dreaming*, Jacqueline Woodson
*Cry the Beloved Country*, Alan Paton
*Crying in H Mart*, Michelle Zauner
*Everything Sad is Untrue*, Daniel Nayeri
*Finding Me*, Viola Davis
*The Girl With the Seven Names*, Hyeonseo Lee
*Go Back to Where You Came From*, Wajahat Ali
*Here We Are: American Dreams, American Nightmares*, Aarti Namdev Shah
*Homegoing*, Yaa Gayasi
*The House of Belonging*, David Whyte
*I Take My Coffee Black*, Tyler Merritt
*A Long Way Home*, Saroo Brierley
*Minor Feelings*, Cathy Park Hong
*The Namesake*, Jhumpa Lahiri
*Solito*, Javier Zamora
*They Poured Fire on Us From the Sky*, Alephonsion Deng, Benson Deng, and Benjamin Ajak
*This Here Flesh*, Cole Arthur Riley
*Touch the Earth: Poems on the Way*, Drew Jackson
*The Ungrateful Refugee*, Dina Nayeri
*What My Bones Know*, Stephanie Foo
*You Bring the Distant Near*, Mitali Perkins

# NOTES

## INTRODUCTION: A COUNTRY WITH NO NAME

[1]Material from the introduction has been adapted from Prasanta Verma, "A Country with No Name: Living in Liminal Spaces," Asian American Christian Collaborative, March 23, 2021, www.asianamericanchristiancollaborative.com /article/a-country-with-no-name-living-in-liminal-spaces. Used with permission.

## 1. DEFINING ETHNIC LONELINESS

[1]UCLA has a "loneliness scale," which measures feelings of loneliness and social isolation. See https://fetzer.org/sites/default/files/images/stories/pdf/self measures/Self_Measures_for_Loneliness_and_Interpersonal_Problems _UCLA_LONELINESS.pdf.

[2]Fay Bound Alberti, *A Biography of Loneliness: The History of an Emotion* (New York: Oxford University Press, 2019), 6.

[3]Christina Ianzito, "U.S. Surgeon General Vivek Murthy on the Dangers of Loneliness," AARP, June 6, 2020, www.aarp.org/health/healthy-living/info-2020 /vivek-murthy-loneliness.html.

[4]Vivek H. Murthy, MD, *Together: The Healing Power of Human Connection in a Sometimes Lonely World* (New York: HarperCollins, 2020), 8.

[5]Vivek Murthy, "Work and the Loneliness Epidemic," *Harvard Business Review*, September 26, 2017, https://hbr.org/2017/09/work-and-the-loneliness-epidemic.

[6]Murthy, *Our Epidemic of Loneliness and Isolation*.

[7]Ryan Jenkins, "How Does the Brain React to Loneliness," *Psychology Today*, March 8, 2022, www.psychologytoday.com/au/blog/the-case-connection/202203 /how-does-the-brain-react-loneliness.

[8]John T. Cacioppo, James H. Fowler, and Nicholas A. Christakis, "Alone in the Crowd: The Structure and Spread of Loneliness in a Large Social Network," *Journal of Personality and Social Psychology* 97, no. 6 (2009): 977-91, https://doi .org/10.1037/a0016076.

[9]Daniel Cox, "The State of American Friendship: Change, Challenges, and Loss," Survey Center on American Life, June 8, 2021, www.americansurveycenter.org /research/the-state-of-american-friendship-change-challenges-and-loss/.

[10] Richard Weissbourd, Milena Batanova, Virginia Lovison, and Eric Torres, *Loneliness in America: How the Pandemic Has Deepened an Epidemic of Loneliness and What We Can Do About It*, Making Caring Common Project, Harvard Graduate School of Education, February 2021, https://mcc.gse.harvard.edu /reports/loneliness-in-america.

[11] Murthy, *Our Epidemic of Loneliness and Isolation*, 8-9.

[12] Alberti, *A Biography of Loneliness*, x.

[13] John Sundholm, "Grocery Chain Started a 'Chat Checkout' Lane for Lonely Seniors Who Need a Friend," Yahoo! News, July 14, 2023, https://news.yahoo.com /grocery-chain-started-chat-checkout-091500925.html#:~:text=Dutch%20 chain%20Jumbo%20has%20a.

[14] Meghan O'Rourke, *The Invisible Kingdom: Reimagining Chronic Illness* (New York: Riverhead Books, 2022), 7.

[15] "Global Population—Distribution by Continent 2022," Statista (Statista Research Department, October 18, 2022), www.statista.com/statistics/237584 /distribution-of-the-world-population-by-continent/.

[16] Shereen Marisol Meraji, Natalie Escobar, and Kumari Devarajan, "Is It Time to Say R.I.P. To 'POC'?," *Code Switch*, NPR, September 30, 2020, www.npr .org/2020/09/29/918418825/is-it-time-to-say-r-i-p-to-p-o-c.

[17] Paul Starr, "The Re-Emergence of 'People of Color,'" *Du Bois Review: Social Science Research on Race* 20, no. 1 (June 13, 2022): 1-20, https://doi.org/10.1017 /s1742058x22000145.

[18] Robert Chao Romero, *Brown Church* (Downers Grove, IL: InterVarsity Press, 2020), 14-15.

[19] Willie James Jennings, *After Whiteness: An Education in Belonging* (Grand Rapids, MI: Eerdmans, 2020), 9.

[20] "Whiteness," National Museum of African American History and Culture, October 1, 2019, https://nmaahc.si.edu/learn/talking-about-race/topics/whiteness.

[21] Sarah Shin, *Beyond Colorblind: Redeeming Our Ethnic Journey* (Downers Grove, IL: InterVarsity Press, 2017), 13.

[22] Nicki Lisa Cole, "What's the Difference Between Hispanic and Latino?," ThoughtCo, updated May 20, 2021, www.thoughtco.com/hispanic-vs-latino -4149966.

[23] Isabelia Herrera, "Hispanic or Latino?," interview by Michel Martin, *All Things Considered*, NPR, September 22, 2019, www.npr.org/2019/09/22/76323 9805/hispanic-or-latino.

[24] Cole, "What's the Difference?"

[25] Anna Purna Kambhampaty, "In 1968, These Activists Coined the Term 'Asian American'—and Helped Shape Decades of Advocacy," *Time*, May 22, 2020, https://time.com/5837805/asian-american-history/.

[26]Li Zhou, "The Inadequacy of the Term 'Asian American,'" Vox, May 5, 2021, www.vox.com/identities/22380197/asian-american-pacific-islander-aapi -heritage-anti-asian-hate-attacks.

[27]New African, "Don't Call Me African-American," *New African* magazine, May 9, 2012, https://newafricanmagazine.com/3168/.

[28]Cydney Adams, "Not All Black People Are African American. Here's the Difference.," CBS News, June 18, 2020, www.cbsnews.com/news/not-all -black-people-are-african-american-what-is-the-difference/.

[29]Erika V. Hall, Sarah S. M. Townsend, and James T. Carter, "Black or African American: Does the History of a Racial Label Affect What That Label Says About Me?" *Character & Context* blog, Society for Personality and Social Psychology, March 23, 2022, https://spsp.org/news-center/character-context-blog /black-or-african-american-does-history-racial-label-affect-what.

[30]Lydia Saad, "Gallup Vault: Black Americans' Preferred Racial Label," Gallup, July 13, 2020, https://news.gallup.com/vault/315566/gallup-vault-black-americans -preferred-racial-label.aspx.

[31]John Eligon, "A Debate over Identity and Race Asks, Are African-Americans 'Black' or 'black'?," *New York Times*, June 26, 2020, www.nytimes.com/2020 /06/26/us/black-african-american-style-debate.html.

[32]Virginia Gorlinski, *Encylcopedia Britannica Online*, s.v. "bhangra," updated May 12, 2023, www.britannica.com/art/bhangra.

[33]Jacqueline A. Bussie, *Love Without Limits: Jesus' Radical Vision for Love with No Exceptions* (Minneapolis, MN: Broadleaf Books, 2022), 168-69.

## 2. DISBELONGING AND HOME

[1]Mona Chalabi, "How Many Times Does the Average Person Move?," FiveThirtyEight, January 29, 2015, https://fivethirtyeight.com/features/how -many-times-the-average-person-moves/.

[2]"Chapter 1: The Nation's Immigration Laws, 1920 to Today," in *Modern Immigration Wave Brings 59 Million to U.S., Driving Population Growth and Change Through 2065: Views of Immigration's Impact on U.S. Society*, Pew Research Center, September 28, 2015, www.pewresearch.org/hispanic/2015/09/28 /chapter-1-the-nations-immigration-laws-1920-to-today/.

[3]Jane Hong, "Op-Ed: The Law That Created Illegal Immigration," *Los Angeles Times*, October 2, 2015, www.latimes.com/opinion/op-ed/la-oe-1002-hong -1965-immigration-act-20151002-story.html.

[4]Abby Budiman, "Key Findings about U.S. Immigrants," Pew Research Center, August 20, 2020, www.pewresearch.org/short-reads/2020/08/20/key-findings -about-u-s-immigrants/.

[5]Our Changing Population: United States," USA Facts, updated July 2022, https://usafacts.org/data/topics/people-society/population-and-demographics/our-changing-population/.

[6]"U.S. Census Bureau Projections Show a Slower Growing, Older, More Diverse Nation a Half Century from Now," United States Census Bureau, December 12, 2012, www.census.gov/newsroom/releases/archives/population/cb12-243.html.

[7]Lesley Kennedy, "How the Immigration Act of 1965 Changed the Face of America," History.com, August 12, 2019, www.history.com/news/immigration-act-1965-changes.

[8]Jonathan Vespa, Lauren Medina, and David Armstrong, *Demographic Turning Points for the United States: Population Projections for 2020 to 2060: Population Estimates and Projections Current Population Reports*," revised February 2020, www.census.gov/content/dam/Census/library/publications/2020/demo/p25-1144.pdf.

[9]Vespa, Medina, and Armstrong, *Demographic Turning Points for the United States*.

[10]Vespa, Medina, and Armstrong, *Demographic Turning Points for the United States*.

[11]Jason Devine, "We Are a Changing Nation: A Series on Population Trends," United States Census Bureau, August 9, 2017, www.census.gov/library/stories/2017/08/changing-nation-demographic-trends.html.

[12]Abby Budiman and Neil G. Ruiz, "Asian Americans Are the Fastest-Growing Racial or Ethnic Group in the U.S.," Pew Research Center, April 9, 2021, www.pewresearch.org/short-reads/2021/04/09/asian-americans-are-the-fastest-growing-racial-or-ethnic-group-in-the-u-s/.

[13]"Hispanic Population to Reach 111 Million by 2060," United States Census Bureau, October 4, 2018, www.census.gov/library/visualizations/2018/comm/hispanic-projected-pop.html.

[14]Adrian Pei, *The Minority Experience: Navigating Emotional and Organizational Realities* (Downers Grove, IL: InterVarsity Press, 2018), 13.

[15]Pei, *The Minority Experience*, 54.

[16]Catherine McNeil, *Fearing Bravely: Risking Love for Our Neighbors, Strangers, and Enemies* (Colorado Springs, CO: NavPress, 2022), 99.

[17]Alberti, *A Biography of Loneliness*, 13.

[18]Alberti, *A Biography of Loneliness*, 172.

[19]Natasha Sistrunk Robinson, *A Sojourner's Truth: Choosing Freedom and Courage in a Divided World* (Downers Grove, IL: InterVarsity Press, 2018), 39.

[20]Andy Crouch, *The Life We're Looking For* (New York: Convergent Books, 2022), 154-55.

[21]Alberti, *A Biography of Loneliness*, 149, 157.

[22]D'Vera Cohn et al., *Financial Issues Top the List of Reasons U.S. Adults Live in Multigenerational Homes*, Pew Research Center's Social & Demographic Trends Project, March 24, 2022, www.pewresearch.org/social-trends/2022/03/24/the-experiences-of-adults-in-multigenerational-households/.

[23]David P. Leong, *Race and Place: How Urban Geography Shapes the Journey to Reconciliation* (Downers Grove, IL: InterVarsity Press, 2017), 35.

[24]Leong, *Race and Place*, 114.

[25]Willie James Jennings, *The Christian Imagination: Theology and the Origins of Race* (New Haven, CT: Yale University Press, 2010), 287-89.

[26]Nate Silver, "The Most Diverse Cities Are Often the Most Segregated," FiveThirtyEight, May 2015, https://fivethirtyeight.com/features/the-most-diverse-cities-are-often-the-most-segregated/.

[27]George Ella Lyon, "Where I'm From," George Ella Lyon, Writer & Teacher, 2010, www.georgeellalyon.com/where.html.

## 3. BEAUTY, BELONGING, AND IDENTITY THEFT

[1]Chanequa Walker-Barnes, *I Bring the Voices of My People: A Womanist Vision for Racial Reconciliation* (Grand Rapids, MI: Eerdmans, 2019), 85.

[2]Walker-Barnes, *I Bring the Voices of My People*, 85.

[3]Walker-Barnes, *I Bring the Voices of My People*, 86, 94-95.

[4]Sakshi Venkatraman, "Iconic Bollywood Film Adapted for Broadway Whitewashed Lead Character. Fans Aren't Happy.," NBC News, August 2, 2022, www.nbcnews.com/news/asian-america/new-ddlj-musical-cast-white-man-lead-fans-arent-happy-rcna41027.

[5]Que-Lam Huynh, Thierry Devos, and Laura Smalarz, "Perpetual Foreigner in One's Own Land: Potential Implications for Identity and Psychological Adjustment," *Journal of Social and Clinical Psychology* 30, no. 2 ( February 2011), 133-62, www.researchgate.net/publication/51127383_Perpetual_Foreigner_in_One%27s_Own_Land_Potential_Implications_for_Identity_and_Psychological_Adjustment.

[6]Chandra Crane, *Mixed Blessing: Embracing the Fullness of Your Multiethnic Identity* (Downers Grove, IL: InterVarsity Press, 2020), 4.

[7]"What Census Calls Us," Pew Research Center, February 6, 2020, www.pewresearch.org/interactives/what-census-calls-us/.

[8]Harvard Radcliffe Institute, "Book Talk with Meghan O'Rourke," YouTube, August 1, 2022, www.youtube.com/watch?v=hWA-GBX6Ae4.

[9]Meghan O'Rourke, *The Invisible Kingdom: Reimagining Chronic Illness* (New York: Riverhead Books, 2022), 6-7.

[10] Geoffrey L. Cohen, *Belonging: The Science of Creating Connection and Bridging Divides* (New York: W. W. Norton & Company, 2022), 160.

[11] Valarie Kaur, *See No Stranger: A Memoir and Manifesto of Revolutionary Love* (New York: One World, 2020), 11.

[12] John, O'Donohue, *Anam Cara: A Book of Celtic Wisdom* (New York: Harper-Collins, 1997), xviii.

[13] Sahaj Kaur Kohli, "Stop Telling Me to Be Authentic," *Culturally Enough*, July 5, 2023, https://culturallyenough.substack.com/p/stop-telling-me-to-be-authentic.

[14] Dan P. McAdams and Fred B. Bryant, "Intimacy Motivation and Subjective Mental Health in a Nationwide Sample," *Journal of Personality* 55, no. 3 (September 1987): 395-413, https://doi.org/10.1111/j.1467-6494.1987.tb00444.x.

[15] Craig Thompson, "There Are More International Students in the US than Ever Before—How Many Get to See the Inside of an American Home?," *Clearing Customs*, November 21, 2018, https://clearingcustoms.net/2018/11/21/there-are-more-international-students-in-the-us-than-ever-before-how-many-get-to-see-the-inside-of-an-american-home/.

[16] Brenda Salter McNeil and Rick Richardson, *The Heart of Racial Justice: How Soul Change Leads to Social Change* (Downers Grove, IL: InterVarsity Press, 2022), 34.

[17] "Ger," Old Testament Hebrew Lexicon - New American Standard, Bible Study Tools, accessed July 3, 2023, www.biblestudytools.com/lexicons/hebrew/nas/ger.html.

[18] Ronald Rolheiser, *The Holy Longing: The Search for a Christian Spirituality* (New York: Image, 2019), 64-65.

[19] Rolheiser, *The Holy Longing*, 66.

[20] Kaur, *See No Stranger*, 43.

[21] E. Randolph Richards and Brandon J. O'Brien, *Misreading Scripture with Western Eyes* (Downers Grove, IL: InterVarsity Press, 2012).

[22] J. I. Packer, *Knowing God* (Downers Grove, IL: InterVarsity Press, 1973), 41-42.

## 4. ISOLATED AND OTHERED

[1] Chimamanda Ngozi Adichie, "The Danger of a Single Story," TED, YouTube, October 7, 2009, www.youtube.com/watch?v=D9Ihs241zeg.

[2] Sarah Shin, *Beyond Colorblind: Redeeming Our Ethnic Journey* (Downers Grove, IL: InterVarsity Press, 2022), 10.

[3] Chandra Crane, *Mixed Blessing: Embracing the Fullness of Your Multiethnic Identity* (Downers Grove, IL: InterVarsity Press, 2020), 54.

[4]"Children Notice Race Several Years Before Adults Want to Talk About It," American Psychological Association, August 27, 2020, www.apa.org/news /press/releases/2020/08/children-notice-race.

[5]Adriana Rezal, "The Racial Makeup of America's Prisons," U.S. News & World Report, October 13, 2021, www.usnews.com/news/best-states/articles/2021-10-13 /report-highlights-staggering-racial-disparities-in-us-incarceration-rates.

[6]David P. Leong, *Race and Place: How Urban Geography Shapes the Journey to Reconciliation* (Downers Grove, IL: InterVarsity Press, 2017), 46.

[7]Church Answers, "Healing Our Racial Divide—An Interview with Dr. Derwin Gray," YouTube, April 5, 2022, www.youtube.com/watch?v=01sQAbi4P48.

[8]Abby Budiman and Neil G. Ruiz, "Asian Americans Are the Fastest-Growing Racial or Ethnic Group in the U.S.," Pew Research Center, April 9, 2021, www.pewresearch.org/short-reads/2021/04/09/asian-americans-are -the-fastest-growing-racial-or-ethnic-group-in-the-u-s/.

[9]Allison Long, "Increased Cases of Social Anxiety Disorder May Be a Lasting Legacy of the COVID-19 Pandemic, Says USF Health Psychiatry Expert— USF Health News," USF Health News, May 10, 2022, https://hscweb3.hsc .usf.edu/blog/2022/05/10/increased-cases-of-social-anxiety-disorder-may -be-a-lasting-legacy-of-the-covid-19-pandemic-says-usf-health-psychiatry -expert/.

[10]Kat Chow, "'Model Minority' Myth Again Used as a Racial Wedge Between Asians and Blacks," *Code Switch*, NPR, April 19, 2017, www.npr.org/sections /codeswitch/2017/04/19/524571669/model-minority-myth-again-used-as-a -racial-wedge-between-asians-and-blacks.

[11]Budiman and Ruiz, "Key Facts About Asian Americans."

[12]Catherine Ceniza Choy, *Asian American Histories of the United States* (Boston: Beacon Press, 2022), xii.

[13]Kimberly Yam, "Asian-Americans Have Highest Poverty Rate in NYC, but Stereotypes Make the Issue Invisible," HuffPost, May 8, 2017, www.huffpost.com /entry/asian-american-poverty-nyc_n_58ff7f40e4b0c46f0782a5b6.

[14]Nichole Argo and Hammad Sheikh, *The Belonging Barometer: The State of Belonging in America*, Over Zero and the Center for Inclusion and Belonging at the American Immigration Council, 2023, 3, 5, https://static1.squarespace.com /static/5f7f1da1ea15cd5bef32169f/t/641b16f74a75495c305d2625/1679496953766 /The+Belonging+Barometer.pdf.

[15]"Immigrants in the United States," American Immigration Council, September 21, 2021, www.americanimmigrationcouncil.org/research/immigrants -in-the-united-states.

[16] Prasanta Verma, "Churches Should Help Normalize Mental Health for Asian Americans," *Sojourners*, June 10, 2021, https://sojo.net/articles/churches -should-help-normalize-mental-health-asian-americans.

[17] AAPA Communication Chair, "New Report: Asian Americans Face Unprecedented Mental Health Concerns Due to the COVID-19 Pandemic and Anti-Asian Hate," Asian American Psychological Association, May 27, 2021, https:// aapaonline.org/2021/05/new-report-asian-americans-face-unprecedented -mental-health-concerns-due-to-the-covid-19-pandemic-and-anti-asian-hate/.

[18] "Why Asian Americans Don't Seek Help for Mental Illness," Mass General Brigham McLean, May 10, 2021, www.mcleanhospital.org/essential/why-asian -americans-dont-seek-help-mental-illness.

[19] Quoted in Verma, "Churches Should Help Normalize."

[20] Amelia Noor-Oshiro, "Asian American Young Adults Are the Only Racial Group with Suicide as Their Leading Cause of Death, so Why Is No One Talking about This?," The Conversation, April 23, 2021, https://theconversation .com/asian-american-young-adults-are-the-only-racial-group-with-suicide-as -their-leading-cause-of-death-so-why-is-no-one-talking-about-this-158030.

[21] Angie Hong, Parenting and Twitter Thread, interview by Prasanta Verma, January 27, 2023.

[22] Angie Hong (@angiekayhong), "Reflecting on the continued feeling of a perpetual foreigner," Twitter, January 18, 2023, https://twitter.com/angiekayhong /status/1615760863545405446.

[23] N. T. Wright, Esau McCaulley, David P. Seemuth, and Jennifer Loop, "Ethnicity, Justice, and the People of God: An Exploration into a Biblical Theology of Justice," Udemy, March 2022, www.udemy.com/course/ethnicity-justice -and-the-people-of-god/.

[24] Angie Hong, Parenting and Twitter Thread, interview by Prasanta Verma, January 27, 2023.

[25] Rachel Hatzipanagos, "Adoption Across Races: 'I Know My Parents Love Me, but They Don't Love My People,'" *Seattle Times*, December 13, 2021, www .seattletimes.com/nation-world/nation/adoption-across-races-i-know-my -parents-love-me-but-they-dont-love-my-people/.

[26] This section is adapted from Prasanta Verma, "See, Say, Spell, Repeat," *The Mudroom*, June 4, 2018, https://mudroomblog.com/see-say-spell-repeat/. Used with permission.

[27] Jhumpa Lahiri, *The Namesake* (New York: Mariner Books, 2004), 98.

[28] Karen Yin, "Drop the Hyphen in 'Asian American,'" Conscious Style Guide, January 24, 2018, https://consciousstyleguide.com/drop-hyphen-asian-american/.

[29] Marian Chia-Ming Liu, "What Counts as an 'American Name' in a Changing Nation," *Washington Post*, March 16, 2023, www.washingtonpost.com/nation /interactive/2023/common-american-names-changing/.

[30] Judie Haynes, "7 Naming Customs from Around the World," *TESOL Blog*, July 30, 2015, http://blog.tesol.org/7-naming-customs-from-around-the-world/.

[31] Sabrina S. Chan, Linson Daniel, E. David De Leon, La Thao, *Learning Our Names: Asian American Christians on Identity, Relationships, and Vocation* (Downers Grove, IL: InterVarsity Press, 2022), 10.

[32] Dr. Beverly Lanzetta, "Session 3: Desiring God for God's Own Sake," The Cloud of Unknowing, 1, https://themonkwithin.net/the-cloud-of-unknowing/.

[33] Karen González, *The God Who Sees* (Harrisonburg, VA: Herald Press, 2019), 74.

## 5. MARGINALIZED AND STRANDED

[1] The Harvard Project Implicit Association Test (IAT) can be found here: https:// implicit.harvard.edu/implicit/takeatest.html.

[2] "Our Story," Othering & Belonging Institute, University of California, Berkeley, accessed July 11, 2023, https://belonging.berkeley.edu/our-story.

[3] Sonia Cavazos, "Easter Sunday: A Milestone for Filipino Representation in Film," *Sampan*, September 8, 2022, https://sampan.org/2022/leisure /easter-sunday-a-milestone-for-filipino-representation-in-film/.

[4] Pearl Lo, "Where Is the Outrage over Angelo Quinto's Murder?," *Diverse: Issues in Higher Education*, March 8, 2021, www.diverseeducation.com /demographics/asian-american-pacific-islander/article/15108780/where-is -the-outrage-over-angelo-quintos-murder.

[5] Mandalit del Barco, "Latinos Continue to Be Invisible in Hollywood and the Media, a New Report Finds," NPR, October 6, 2022, www.npr.org/2022/10/06/112723 4498/latinos-continue-to-be-invisible-in-hollywood-and-the-media-a-new -report-finds.

[6] Nancy Wang Yuen, *Reel Inequality: Hollywood Actors and Racism* (New Brunswick, NJ: Rutgers University Press, 2017), 64.

[7] James Tager and Clarisse Rosaz Shariyf, *Reading Between the Lines: Race, Equity, and Book Publishing*, PEN America, October 21, 2022, https://pen.org/report /race-equity-and-book-publishing/?mc_cid=a100a69035&mc_eid=3fe699a4e9.

[8] O'Donohue, *Anam Cara*, 64.

[9] Quoted in Jacqueline A. Bussie, *Love Without Limits: Jesus' Radical Vision for Love with No Exceptions* (Minneapolis, MN: Broadleaf Books, 2022), 23.

[10] Marlena Graves, *The Way Up is Down: Becoming Yourself by Forgetting Yourself* (Downers Grove, IL: InterVarsity Press, 2020).

[11]"Pakistani Woman Killed by Ex-Husband in US over Opening up about Her Divorce Journey on Social Media," *Tribune India*, updated July 24, 2022, www .tribuneindia.com/news/world/pakistani-woman-killed-by-ex-husband-in -us-over-opening-up-about-her-divorce-journey-on-social-media-415269# google_vignette.

[12]"Why the Majority of the World's Poor Are Women," Oxfam International, October 8, 2019, www.oxfam.org/en/why-majority-worlds-poor-are-women.

[13]"Violence Against Women," World Health Organization, March 9, 2021, www .who.int/news-room/fact-sheets/detail/violence-against-women.

[14]"Statistics on Violence Against API Women," Asian Pacific Institute on Gender-Based Violence, 2017, www.api-gbv.org/about-gbv/statistics-violence -against-api-women/.

[15]Katherine Kam, "Why Domestic Violence Calls Are Surging for Asian American Women amid the Pandemic," NBC News, October 1, 2020, www .nbcnews.com/news/asian-america/why-domestic-violence-calls-are-surging -asian-american-women-amid-n1240663.

[16]Emiko Petrosky et al., "Racial and Ethnic Differences in Homicides of Adult Women and the Role of Intimate Partner Violence—United States, 2003–2014," *Morbidity and Mortality Weekly Report* 66, no. 28 (July 21, 2017): 741-46, https://doi.org/10.15585/mmwr.mm6628a1.

[17]"Domestic Violence Against American Indian and Alaska Native Women," National Coalition Against Domestic Violence, 2016, accessed July 7, 2023, https://assets.speakcdn.com/assets/2497/american_indian_and_alaskan_native _women__dv.pdf.

[18]Deborah M. Capaldi et al., "A Systematic Review of Risk Factors for Intimate Partner Violence," *Partner Abuse* 3, no. 2 (2012): 231-80, https://doi .org/10.1891/1946-6560.3.2.231.

[19]"Dietrich Bonhoeffer, "Who Am I?" in *Letters & Papers From Prison* (New York: Touchstone, 1997), 347-48.

## 6. EXILED AND DISCONNECTED

[1]Nichole Argo and Hammad Sheikh, *The Belonging Barometer: The State of Belonging in America*, Over Zero and the Center for Inclusion and Belonging at the American Immigration Council, 2023, 3, 5, https://static1.squarespace.com /static/5f7f1da1ea15cd5bef32169f/t/641b16f74a75495c305d2625/1679496953766 /The+Belonging+Barometer.pdf.

[2]Dr. Mark Mayfield, *The Path Out of Loneliness: Finding and Fostering Connection to God, Ourselves, and One Another* (Colorado Springs, CO: NavPress, 2021), 107.

[3] Shir Atzil and Maria Gendron, "Bio-Behavioral Synchrony Promotes the Development of Conceptualized Emotions," *Current Opinion in Psychology* 17 (October 2017): 162-69, https://doi.org/10.1016/j.copsyc.2017.07.009.

[4] Vanessa Van Edwards, "Mirroring Body Language: 4 Steps to Successfully Mirror Others," Science of People, accessed July 3, 2023, www.scienceofpeople .com/mirroring/.

[5] Allison Long, "Increased Cases of Social Anxiety Disorder May Be a Lasting Legacy of the COVID-19 Pandemic, Says USF Health Psychiatry Expert," USF Health, May 10, 2022, https://hscweb3.hsc.usf.edu/blog/2022/05/10 /increased-cases-of-social-anxiety-disorder-may-be-a-lasting-legacy-of-the -covid-19-pandemic-says-usf-health-psychiatry-expert/.

[6] Mayfield, *The Path Out of Loneliness*, 2-3.

[7] C. S. Lewis, *The Problem of Pain* (New York: Harper Collins, 1996), 91.

[8] Cited in Catherine McNeil, *Fearing Bravely: Risking Love for Our Neighbors, Strangers, and Enemies* (Colorado Springs, CO: NavPress, 2022), 54.

[9] Crouch, *The Life We're Looking For*, 26.

[10] Crouch, *The Life We're Looking For*, 28-29, 58-59.

[11] Sara Konrath, "Speaking of Psychology: The Decline of Empathy and the Rise of Narcissism, with Sara Konrath, PhD" *Speaking of Psychology* podcast, American Psychological Association, APA.org, 2022, www.apa.org/news/podcasts /speaking-of-psychology/empathy-narcissism.

[12] John Scott, "Decline in Human Empathy Creates Global Risks in the 'Age of Anger,'" Zurich, *Financial Times*, accessed July 3, 2023, https://biggerpicture .ft.com/digital-data-and-cyber/article/decline-human-empathy-creates -global-risks-age-anger.

[13] Thomas F. Pettigrew and Linda R. Tropp, "How Does Intergroup Contact Reduce Prejudice? Meta-Analytic Tests of Three Mediators," *European Journal of Social Psychology* 38, no. 6 (September 2008): 922–34, https://doi.org/10.1002 /ejsp.504.

[14] Alan Noble, *You Are Not Your Own: Belonging to God in an Inhuman World* (Downers Grove, IL: InterVarsity Press, 2021), 4.

[15] Noble, *You Are Not Your Own*, 25, 33.

[16] Blaise Pascal, *Pensées* (New York: E. P. Dutton & Co, Inc., 1958; Project Gutenberg, 2017), 40.

[17] Sherry Turkle, *The Empathy Diaries: A Memoir* (New York: Penguin Press, 2021), 334-35.

[18] Kat Armas, *Abuelita Faith: What Women on the Margins Teach Us About Wisdom, Persistence, and Strength* (Grand Rapids, MI: Brazos Press, 2021), 171-72.

[19]Ben Guarino, "Researchers Invent Camouflaged Membrane That Hides like an Octopus," *Washington Post*, October 12, 2017, www.washingtonpost.com/news /speaking-of-science/wp/2017/10/12/researchers-invent-camouflaged-membrane -that-hides-like-an-octopus/.

[20]Taylyn Washington-Harmon, "This Survival Tactic Many BIPOC Use Could Be Harmful to Their Mental Health," Health, May 23, 2022, www.health.com /mind-body/health-diversity-inclusion/code-switching.

## 7. TRAUMA AND HEALING

[1]Effua E. Sosoo, Donte L. Bernard, and Enrique W. Neblett, "The Influence of Internalized Racism on the Relationship Between Discrimination and Anxiety," *Cultural Diversity and Ethnic Minority Psychology* 26, no. 4 (December 30, 2019), https://doi.org/10.1037/cdp0000320.

[2]Xochitl Dixon, "Resisting Assimilation, Embracing ALL of Me," *Brownicity*, September 22, 2022, https://brownicity.com/blog/resisting-assimilation -embracing-all-of-me/.

[3]David L. Eng and Shinhee Han, *Racial Melancholia, Racial Dissociation: On the Social and Psychic Lives of Asian Americans* (Durham, NC: Duke University Press, 2019).

[4]Eng and Han, *Racial Melancholia, Racial Dissociation*, 35, 42-44.

[5]Eng and Han, *Racial Melancholia, Racial Dissociation*, 38, 43.

[6]Rich Villodas, *The Deeply Formed Life: Five Transformative Values to Root Us in the Way of Jesus* (Colorado Springs, CO: WaterBrook, 2020), 104.

[7]Valarie Kaur, *See No Stranger: A Memoir and Manifesto of Revolutionary Love* (New York: One World, 2020), 17.

[8]Willie James Jennings, *After Whiteness: An Education in Belonging* (Grand Rapids, MI: Eerdmans, 2020), 35.

[9]"What Is Epigenetics?," Centers for Disease Control and Prevention, August 15, 2022, www.cdc.gov/genomics/disease/epigenetics.htm.

[10]Rachel Yehuda, "How Parents' Trauma Leaves Biological Traces in Children," *Scientific American* 127, no. 1 (July 1, 2022), https://doi.org/10.1038 /scientificamerican0722-50.

[11]"Racial Trauma," PTSD: National Center for PTSD, U.S. Department of Veteran Affairs, accessed July 3, 2023, www.ptsd.va.gov/understand/types /racial_trauma.asp.

[12]Jenny Guidi, Marcella Lucente, Nicoletta Sonino, Giovanni A. Fava, "Allostatic Load and Its Impact on Health: A Systematic Review," *Psychotherapy and Psychosomatics* 90, no. 1 (December 28, 2020): 11-27, https://doi.org/10.1159/000510696.

[13] Martin Taylor, "What Does Fight, Flight, Freeze, Fawn Mean?," WebMD, April 28, 2022, www.webmd.com/mental-health/what-does-fight-flight-freeze -fawn-mean.

[14] "Exhibit 1.3-4: DSM-5 Diagnostic Criteria for PTSD," Substance Abuse and Mental Health Services Administration, 2014, www.ncbi.nlm.nih.gov/books /NBK207191/box/part1_ch3.box16/.

[15] "How Common Is PTSD in Adults?," PTSD: National Center for PTSD, U.S. Department of Veteran Affairs, 2014, www.ptsd.va.gov/understand/common /common_adults.asp.

[16] Monnica T. Williams, "Can Racism Cause PTSD? Implications for DSM-5," *Psychology Today* blog, May 20, 2013, www.psychologytoday.com/us/blog /culturally-speaking/201305/can-racism-cause-ptsd-implications-dsm-5.

[17] Nnamdi Pole, Suzanne R. Best, Thomas Metzler, and Charles R. Marmar, "Why Are Hispanics at Greater Risk for PTSD?," *Cultural Diversity and Ethnic Minority Psychology* 11, no. 2 (2005): 144-61, https://doi.org/10.1037/1099-9809.11.2.144.

[18] "Native and Indigenous Communities and Mental Health," Mental Health America, 2020, www.mhanational.org/issues/native-and-indigenous-commu nities-and-mental-health.

[19] Kathleen Brown-Rice, "Examining the Theory of Historical Trauma among Native Americans," *The Professional Counselor* 3, no. 3 (October 15, 2014), https://tpcjournal .nbcc.org/examining-the-theory-of-historical-trauma-among-native-americans/.

[20] "Tips for Disaster Responders: Understanding Historical Trauma and Resil- ience When Responding to an Event in Indian Country," Substance Abuse and Mental Health Services Administration, accessed September 18, 2023, https://store.samhsa.gov/sites/default/files/SAMHSA_Digital_Download/pep 22-01-01-005.pdf.

[21] Ehsan Popalzai and Ivana Kottasová, "Taliban Suspend University Education for Women in Afghanistan," CNN, December 20, 2022, www.cnn.com/2022/12/20 /asia/taliban-bans-women-university-education-intl/index.html.

[22] Madeleine L'Engle, *Walking on Water: Reflections on Faith and Art* (New York: Convergent Books, 2016), 88.

[23] This is not meant to serve as medical advice and readers are advised to consult their health care providers.

[24] Kirsten Powers, *Saving Grace: Speak Your Truth, Stay Centered, and Learn to Co- exist with People Who Drive You Nut*s (New York: Convergent, 2021), 122.

[25] J. S. Park, *The Voices We Carry: Finding Your One True Voice in a Clamor of Noise* (Chicago: Northfield Publishing, 2020), 21.

[26] Frederick Buechner, *Wishful Thinking: A Theological ABC* (New York: Harper & Row, 1973), 34.

[27] Anneliese A. Singh, *The Racial Healing Handbook* (Oakland, CA: New Harbinger Publications, 2019).

[28] J. Drew Lanham, "Joy Is the Justice We Give Ourselves," *Emergence Magazine*, August 31, 2022, https://emergencemagazine.org/poem/joy-is-the-justice -we-give-ourselves/.

## 8. SHARING OUR STORIES

[1] Shannan Martin, *Start with Hello: And Other Simple Ways to Live as Neighbors* (Grand Rapids, MI: Revell, 2022), 32.

[2] Adrian Pei, *The Minority Experience: Navigating Emotional and Organizational Realities* (Downers Grove, IL: InterVarsity Press, 2018), 5.

[3] Martin, *Start with Hello*, 56.

[4] Elizabeth Barrett Browning, *Aurora Leigh: A Poem* (London: J. Miller, 1864; Chicago: Academy Chicago Printers, 1979), https://digital.library.upenn.edu /women/barrett/aurora/aurora.html.

[5] Latasha Morrison (@latashamorrison), "If one part suffers," Instagram, June 4, 2020, www.instagram.com/p/CBBZuI6Bv0u/?img_index=1.

[6] Matt Gonzales, "CROWN Act: Does Your State Prohibit Hair Discrimination?," Society for Human Resource Management, February 7, 2023, www.shrm.org /resourcesandtools/hr-topics/behavioral-competencies/global-and-cultural -effectiveness/pages/crown-act-does-your-state-prohibit-hair-discrimination. aspx#:~:text=As%20of%20June%202023%2C%2022.

[7] Kathy Khang, *Raise Your Voice: Why We Stay Silent and How to Speak Up* (Downers Grove, IL: InterVarsity Press, 2018), 3, 10.

[8] Brené Brown, *Braving the Wilderness: The Quest for True Belonging and the Courage to Stand Alone* (New York: Random House, 2017), 53.

[9] Brown, *Braving the Wilderness*, 65.

[10] Dina Nayeri, *The Ungrateful Refugee: What Immigrants Never Tell You* (New York: Catapult, 2019).

[11] "More Animal Main Characters than Non-White People in Children's Books," CBBC, November 11, 2020, www.bbc.co.uk/newsround/54900501.

[12] Quoted in Warren Cole Smith, "C. S. Lewis, Madeleine L'Engle, and the Power of Storytelling," The Rabbit Room, November 29, 2018, https://rabbitroom .com/2018/11/c-s-lewis-madeline-lengle-and-the-power-of-storytelling/.

[13] Eric Costanzo, Daniel Yang, and Matthew Soerens, *Inalienable: How Marginalized Kingdom Voices Can Help Save the American Church* (Downers Grove, IL: InterVarsity Press, 2022), 21-22, 32.

[14] Brown, *Braving the Wilderness*, 158.

## 9. FROM DISBELONGING TO BELONGING

[1]Martha Brettschneider, "Redwoods, Roots, and the Power of Connection," Damselwings, LLC, October 6, 2018, https://damselwings.com/2018/10/06 /redwoods-roots-power-of-connection/.

[2]Richard Grant, "Do Trees Talk to Each Other?," *Smithsonian Magazine*, February 21, 2018, www.smithsonianmag.com/science-nature/the-whispering-trees -180968084/.

[3]Peter Wohlleben, *The Hidden Life of Trees: What They Feel, How They Communicate—Discoveries From a Secret World* (Vancouver, Canada: Greystone Books, 2016).

[4]Erin Alberty, "Utah's Pando Aspen Grove Is the Most Massive Living Thing Known on Earth. It May Die Soon.," *Salt Lake Tribune*, November 14, 2017, www.sltrib.com/news/2017/11/11/utahs-pando-aspen-grove-is-the-most -massive-living-thing-known-on-earth-it-may-die-soon/.

[5]Martin Luther King Jr., "Letter from a Birmingham Jail," African Studies Center, University of Pennsylvania, April 16, 1963, www.africa.upenn.edu/Articles _Gen/Letter_Birmingham.html.

[6]Brené Brown, *Braving the Wilderness: The Quest for True Belonging and the Courage to Stand Alone* (New York: Random House, 2017), 130.

[7]Viola Davis, "Courage and Power from Pain: An Interview with Viola Davis" interview by Brené Brown, *Braving the Wilderness* (New York: Random House, 2017) 86-87.

[8]Mark Nepo, *More Together Than Alone: Discovering the Power and Spirit of Community in Our Lives and in the World* (New York: Atria Books, 2018), 19.

[9]Brown, *Braving the Wilderness*, 151.

[10]Pete Scazzero, "Session 2: Know Yourself That You May Know God," Emotionally Healthy Spirituality," accessed July 3, 2023, 2, www.emotionallyhealthy .org/wp-content/uploads/2015/10/Session-2-Know-Yourself-Know-God.pdf.

[11]Dorothy Day, *The Long Loneliness: The Autobiography of the Legendary Catholic Social Activist* (New York: HarperOne, 2017).

[12]Dietrich Bonhoeffer, *Life Together: A Discussion of Christian Fellowship*, trans. John W. Doberstein (London: SCM Press Ltd, 1954), 15.

[13]Armas, *Abuelita Faith*, 21.

[14]Aaron Williams and Armand Emamdjomeh, "America Is More Diverse than Ever—but Still Segregated," *Washington Post*, May 2, 2018, www.washingtonpost .com/graphics/2018/national/segregation-us-cities/.

[15]*Merriam-Webster*, s.v. "xenophobia (*n.*)," accessed August 30, 2023, www.merriam -webster.com/dictionary/xenophobia.

[16] Shannan Martin, *Start with Hello: And Other Simple Ways to Live as Neighbors* (Grand Rapids, MI: Revell, 2022), 140.

[17] Armas, *Abuelita Faith*, 171-72.

[18] Brown, *Braving the Wilderness*, 156.

[19] Lauren F. Winner, *Wearing God: Clothing, Laughter, Fire, and Other Overlooked Ways of Meeting God* (New York: HarperOne, 2015), 68.

[20] "Loneliness Can Be Contagious, Study Finds," UChicago News, December 1, 2009, https://news.uchicago.edu/story/loneliness-can-be-contagious-study-finds.

[21] Tim Radford, "Horses Can Recognise Human Emotion, New Study Shows," *The Guardian*, February 10, 2016, www.theguardian.com/science/2016/feb/10 /horses-can-recognise-human-emotion-new-study-shows.

[22] Elizabeth Gamillo, "Mushrooms May Communicate with Each Other Using Electrical Impulses," *Smithsonian Magazine*, April 12, 2022, www.smithsonian mag.com/smart-news/mushrooms-may-communicate-with-each-other-using -electrical-impulses-180979889/.

[23] Dave Davies, "Trees Talk to Each Other. 'Mother Tree' Ecologist Hears Lessons for People, Too," NPR, May 4, 2021, www.npr.org/sections/health-shots/2021/05 /04/993430007/trees-talk-to-each-other-mother-tree-ecologist-hears-lessons -for-people-too.

[24] J. A. C. J. Bastiaansen, M. Thioux, and C. Keysers, "Evidence for Mirror Systems in Emotions," *Philosophical Transactions of the Royal Society B: Biological Sciences* 364, no. 1528 (August 27, 2009): 2391–404, https://doi.org/10.1098 /rstb.2009.0058.

## 10. A BETTER COUNTRY

[1] Kristen Radtke, *Seek You: A Journey Through American Loneliness* (New York: Pantheon Books, 2021), 340.

[2] Diane Langberg, *Suffering and the Heart of God: How Trauma Destroys and Christ Restores* (Greensboro, NC: New Growth Press, 2015), 65.

[3] Austin Channing Brown, *I'm Still Here: Black Dignity in a World Made for Whiteness* (New York: Convergent, 2018), 174.

[4] David Whyte, *Consolations: The Solace, Nourishment and Underlying Meaning of Everyday Words* (Langley, WA: Many Rivers Press, 2015), 131-33.

[5] Quoted in Michael Austi, "Spirituality and Our Humanity: Become More Truly Human," *Psychology Today* blog, December 20, 2020, www.psychologytoday .com/us/blog/ethics-everyone/202012/spirituality-and-our-humanity.

[6] *Strong's Concordance*, s.v. "5381. philoxenia," Bible Hub, accessed September 18, 2023, https://biblehub.com/greek/5381.htm.

[7] Andrew Shryock, quoted by Joe Keohane, "How Humans Came to Rely on the Kindness of Strangers," Big Think, August 2, 2021, https://bigthink.com/the-present/how-humans-rely-kindness-strangers/.

[8] Sarah Reid, "Four Countries with a Tradition of Kindness," BBC, April 13, 2020, www.bbc.com/travel/article/20200412-four-countries-with-a-tradition-of-kindness.

[9] N. T. Wright, Esau McCaulley, David P. Seemuth, and Jennifer Loop, "Ethnicity, Justice, and the People of God: An Exploration into a Biblical Theology of Justice," Udemy, March 2022, www.udemy.com/course/ethnicity-justice-and-the-people-of-god/.

[10] Joanna Ho, *Eyes That Kiss in the Corners* (New York: HarperCollins, 2021).

# ABOUT THE AUTHOR

Prasanta Verma (MBA, MPH) was born under an Asian sun, raised in the Appalachian foothills, and currently resides in the Midwest. Her work has been published in *Sojourners*, *The Curator Magazine*, the *Indianapolis Review*, *Relief Journal*, *The Mudroom* blog, *Guideposts Pray a Word a Day*, and others. In addition to writing, Prasanta served as a speech and debate coach for ten years. When she's not writing or working, she's drinking chai and reading a good book. Prasanta lives in Wisconsin with her family.

Website: www.prasantaverma.com

Twitter: @VermaPrasanta

Instagram: @prasantaverma

Facebook: @prasantavermawriter